SCOTLAND'S TEN TOMORROWS

The Devolution Crisis – and How to Fix It

Edited by Bill Jamieson

continuum
LONDON • NEW YORK

Continuum International Publishing Group
The Tower Building, 11 York Road, London SE1 7NX
80 Maiden Lane, Suite 704, New York NY 10038

www.continuumbooks.com

First published 2006

British Library Cataloguing-in-Publication Data
A catalogue record for this book is available from the British Library.

ISBN: 0–8264–5272–8

Typeset by Kenneth Burnley, Wirral, Cheshire
Printed and bound in Great Britain by MPG Books Ltd, Bodmin, Cornwall

Contents

BILL JAMIESON

Introduction:
How devolution became the
Emperor's new clothes

Scotland's 10 Tomorrows is a publication set to inspire and infuriate in equal measure.

Eight years after devolution, it is the first serious attempt to raise a rebel standard against the resulting relentless growth of government in Scotland and the failure of this approach to raise our aspirations and our prospects.

It will inspire because it is the first attempt to present a critique of devolution outside of the Holyrood government bubble and untainted by apologies, excuses and justifications: the rhetorical dissemblage of the deaf that passes for political discourse in the Scottish Parliament. Here a group of free-thinking writers, outwith the government Leviathan, presents an analysis of what is going wrong and sets out positive, practical and achievable options for change.

It will inspire because, without a penny of public subsidy that slants and confines policy discussion in Scotland to a favoured few, the authors present independent analysis and assessment setting out how change and escape is not only possible, but imperative. How can we progress from here? And what are the options we should consider? Here the authors have come up with a range of ideas and solutions that I hope will make this book a positive contribution to debate about Scotland's future.

It will inspire because it speaks to that other Scotland, the Scotland outside the Holyrood government bubble, the Scotland of proud cities and little towns, that is capable of so much more than the regulatory Leviathan can imagine, still less deliver.

And it will infuriate because it exposes that most corrosive conceit of the Holyrood establishment: that the ruling coalition is set up for life; that there is little possibility of change, that 'this is how it has to be'.

This collection of essays is not an organized programme or manifesto. Each writer has written in a personal capacity. And each comes from different, often opposing perspectives about what has gone wrong and what now needs to change.

As with Scottish public opinion overall, there are contradictory attitudes. Some believe that devolution as we know it is now a fact of life and that those who opposed it need to recant and move on. This is supported by surveys of public opinion showing only a small proportion of voters wanting to see a return to rule from Westminster. However, 59 per cent of Scots also think that standards in key public services should be the same in all parts of the UK.

Others, such as the writer Gerald Warner, see devolution as an issue much wider than health and education provision. Warner brings to his critique all the fiery denunciation of a Scottish Edmund Burke. Devolution, he says, has been a disaster. He views the Scotland Act as the reigning error of policy and a folly which disillusioned Scots cannot and should not bring themselves to embrace.

Still others argue that it is the politics of devolution that needs to change, not the constitutional fact. And across the majority of writers there is concern over the standards of public services and a firm belief that, while devolution provides 'local' choices on spending priorities, a gap in the range and quality of services relative to the rest of the UK is unacceptable. This is a contradiction that will require some navigation to overcome.

But all, from their specialist areas, are united in one regard: the devolution story as it stands has run out of narrative. Change is a necessity if Scotland is to have a fighting chance to be a free and prosperous nation. Without change, it risks becoming a bureaucracy-burdened state in which reform and improvement are frustrated and that other Scotland, of free, voluntary and private institutions and initiative, is squeezed and crowded out.

Scotland is now approaching a critical inflection point. It cannot move forward out of the trough it is in unless it makes fundamental changes in the composition and manner of government. In this sense its predicament may be compared to that of a company in the grip of a yesteryear inventor. The changes necessary to move the company forward are resisted to preserve an order that has outlived its purpose and utility.

How has a country, so proud of its history and culture, and so able and willing to be a vibrant, prosperous nation, come to this? What are the causes of the present discontent? Across the country there is growing disillusion at how devolution has played out: of a poverty of idea and mission and an obsession with the petty while the important is left to lie.

What has gone wrong? One popular dissatisfaction is clear, and it is vocal. There is increasing anger at the way in which Holyrood and the devolved administration at large has turned into a runaway gravy train for the political class. Nothing seems able to slow, still less halt, this runaway train of jobs and perks and goodies. For a time even MSPs themselves were embarrassed and overwhelmed by the debacle of the Holyrood parliament building, of which they were ostensibly in charge. How helpless they seemed as its cost spiralled from some £60 million to more than £430 million before their eyes. But it was not long before the dust settled and the parliament resumed its business, in which two themes were wearisomely familiar: the lack of powers in areas where power matters, in particular the economy; and the mission to expose and expunge 'market failure'.

Market failure? Few seemed aware of the irony that while the parliament was establishing a new record in public procurement failure, the Royal Bank of Scotland had completed a global headquarters on the outskirts of Edinburgh catering for a staff of 300 and featuring *inter alia*: one million square metres of office space set in 100 acres of landscaped woodland, an on-site mini Tesco supermarket, chemist and florist, dentist and doctor, along with a 480-seat terrace restaurant and facilities for barbecues, running and cycling tracks, football pitches and a leisure centre with a swimming pool, gym, and dance and aerobics studios, two Starbucks coffee bars, a crèche for up to 120 pre-school children and, amid the jogging paths and woodland, a training and conference centre with a 300-seat auditorium together with copious overnight accommodation: all this at a cost of some £350 million, or 20 per cent less than the eight-times-over-budget and two-years-late Holyrood parliament. Rather than 'market failure' being the demon, it would seem that public sector procurement has much to learn from it.

But the building was only the start. Across the public at large an exhaustion of parliament numbers has now set in. Latest figures put the annual running costs of the high-maintenance building at £66 million; that the wage bill for MSPs has now crossed £10 million; that annual staff costs are close behind and that the total budget for the parliament in 2006–07 is now in excess of £95 million.

As with the cost of the parliament, many MSPs are embarrassed by these figures. Most expense claims do not go to the extremes. But to say that the rules of the parliament act as a sanction against excess would be to stretch credulity. The party list system by which a large number of MSPs get into parliament without direct accountability to the voters works to reinforce the established party machines and a sense of detachment from the real concerns of voters.

An actual case of automatic 'list' succession provides a telling vignette of the gravy-train syndrome. In January 2005 a Mr Andrew Arbuckle, a Fife councillor, was welcomed into the bosom of the Scottish Parliament as a new Lib Dem MSP. There was no election campaign, no public meetings, doorstep canvassing or competing candidates. Mr Arbuckle slid into the parliament through the smooth, silent machinery of the party list system, automatically replacing his colleague further up the list. This was a Mr Keith Raffan, barely known outside the parliament until three weeks previously when he became headline news with the revelation that he has racked up a record expenses claim of £108,825, a sum that included travel expenses of £41,000.

At the parliament's agreed car mileage rate this would have enabled the MSP for Mid Scotland and Fife to travel three and a half times round the earth in his Skoda Fabia. Mr Arbuckle succeeded to the parliament seat in a process that cut out all opportunity for voters to have a say in the matter. To add a somewhat piquant touch, Mr Arbuckle said on his appointment he would like if possible to retain his place on Fife Council's standards committee.

To dismiss criticism of such a state of affairs as anti devolution or anti-Scottish – now the default riposte of the Executive to any expression of criticism – is surely to deeply misread public disquiet over parliamentary accountability, or the lack of it.

Meanwhile, the aggregate figures for the ongoing cost of the parliament are numbing, just as the building itself numbs the eye and challenges explanation. Two years after its completion, Scots are still struggling to come to terms with how a building of such debatable aesthetics could come to represent the devolution aspiration, never mind to cost so much. Cramped and crimped on an inadequate site, the first impression of a parliament in which so much expectation was vested is one of warring confusion. The distraught angles, the Gothic over-fussiness, the dark, depressing low concrete-ceilinged foyer as if to provide cool relief from the searing Caledonian sun: all this looks faintly ridiculous at the foot of the splendidly Hanseatic Royal Mile. The oriental wood pole-slatted windows (looking directly into a nearby block of flats) and the late additions of the concrete water pistols (or are they hairdryers?) on the sides of the building to relieve the battleship grey cement rendering, complete the impression of a fetishistic hotchpotch of styles intended to create the very dissonance and incongruity that repels so many. Any sense of Scottish vernacular has been expunged. The whole shows a disrespect bordering on contempt for Scottish history, culture and sensibility. In this import of dissonant postmodern Barcelona Gothic for our national parliament many are struck by an intense betrayal of our country and the values that define us as a people.

Yet nothing seems able to break through the obsessive self regard of the Holyrood set, expanding with every year, and an Executive salariat fed and sustained by an ever lengthening caravan of advisers, press officers, policy wonks, researchers, minders and bag-carriers of all sorts. The number of media staff has tripled since 1997 to more than 90 and the annual wage bill for special advisers has leapt more than 75 per cent: all this, it often seems, thrown in to resist improvements and reforms in the two great areas of public policy with which they are exclusively charged: health and education. Much of this opposition appears for no other reason than that change might loosen the timeless grip of North Lanarkshire Stalinism that still pervades so much of the Scottish central belt.

Civil service numbers alone have grown by 51,000 to 577,000 in just four years. On top of this is a 'hidden' public sector workforce of 110,000 comprising doctors, cleaners and caterers somehow omitted from the official count. Then add to this the large number of consultants, accountants, project workers and temporary staff also omitted. Little wonder that half of all Executive spending goes on wages and that government in all its many guises is now the biggest thing going in Scotland.

When the Scottish Parliament came into being, the annual budget of the Executive stood at just over £16 billion. By 2004–05 this had rocketed to £27.4 billion. By the end of 2007 it will have reached more than £30 billion. Put another way, by 2007 the Executive will be spending £117 on every Scot each week – more than many will take home in their pay packets.

Indeed, such is this rate of growth that it seems expansion of government in Scotland is no longer the means to an end, but the endgame itself. In this it seems there has been something akin to an internal coup d'état in which the state has overthrown the previous order to secure an even bigger and more powerful model. Certainly if growth and multiplication of functions was the policy aim, it has succeeded beyond the wildest dreams of its creators.

So those who question why *Scotland's Ten Tomorrows* has appeared or why it is needed may risk missing the point. The wonder is not so much that it is being published now as that it has taken the time that it has. For if this is 'how it has to be', it should surely not come as a surprise that more are coming to question how such a massive increase in Scotland in the machinery, competence, scope and expense of government can yield so little by way of wider benefit and enhanced result.

So great has government expenditure in Scotland become

that it now approximates to some 53 per cent of Gross Domestic Product. Scotland is now placed fourth in a league table of Organisation for Economic Cooperation and Development (OECD) member countries ranked by extent of government activity in the economy. Indeed, we are now marginally ahead of Finland, while England is ten percentage points behind.

For many in government this is not at all a cause for concern but if anything a badge of honour. Indeed, getting public expenditure up to 60 per cent and beyond seems to be the ambition. Certainly the one competence the Scottish Executive has mastered as a skill *par excellence* is its ability to spend other people's money at a ferocious rate and, at the remotest sign that this supply might not continue to arrive from the Treasury at the pace of recent years, to howl about inequity, deprivation and the baleful business of having to juggle priorities like everyone else.

Here there are strong echoes of what the historian **Michael Fry** has eloquently described in his contribution as Scotland 'the victim-nation'. The new Scotland, he writes, is becoming a nation founded on grievance, real or imagined, with a culture not of victors but victims. 'Now she is a victim-nation, able to do nothing for herself, and needing the English or the Europeans to do things for her. Yet perhaps the lessons of history show us that this need not be so.'

So we do not need to look far for the anger in this book. And it is more than an anger of betrayed expectation. It is a betrayal of what Scotland could be, and of her enterprise and pride. The explosion in public expenditure is just not cutting into the problems and grievances that justified the higher than average level of spending per head in Scotland compared to the rest of the UK.

Fraser Nelson, in a blistering paper, sets out some appalling statistics on Scottish life today. For example, for all the vast sums tipped into redistributionist schemes of welfare relief and health improvement, male life expectancy in parts of Glasgow today at 53.9 years is closer to Baghdad (61 years) and closer still to Cameroon (51 years) than the UK average.

Scotland struggles with chronic and growing problems of poor diet, obesity, heart disease, cancer and drug and alcohol addiction. **Gillian Bowditch**, in her paper on NHS Scotland, reports that productivity in the NHS has fallen despite record levels of spending. Out of 14 performance targets set for the service in 2000, only two appear to have been met without qualification four years later.

Meanwhile, despite sustained economic growth across the UK as a whole, Scotland appears to have missed out, with more than 281,000 of working-age Scots on incapacity benefit. As Fraser Nelson calculates, if all of Scotland's invalidity benefit population were to live together, it would outnumber the combined populations of Dunfermline, Falkirk, Kilmarnock, Paisley, Perth and Stirling.

Nowhere has the failure of devolution to 'make a difference' been more stark than in economic performance. Now this failure, it should be said at once, cannot fairly be laid at the door of the Scottish Parliament. Monetary and fiscal policy – the main levers of macro-economic management – firmly remain with the UK government. And it was never a reasonable expectation that devolution would, *per se,* bring economic benefit.

Nevertheless, there was a widely held belief that devolution would boost national self-confidence and aspiration, encourage more to start a business and help raise awareness of Scotland and her economy on the global stage.

And the Scottish Parliament is not totally powerless in the economic realm. It has a massive budget available to it to spend on economic development and infrastructure. In Scottish Enterprise it has one of the biggest public sector economic agencies in Europe with an annual budget of some

£450 million. It has tax-varying powers by way of business rates and the discretion to adjust income tax upwards or downwards by 3p in the pound. And finally it has the commitment of the First Minister Jack McConnell who has repeatedly declared that improving Scotland's economic performance is his 'top priority'.

But what does the record show? Here there is no better informed analysis than that by **George Kerevan** in a powerfully argued paper for this collection. Not only does he deploy statistics with formidable force but one senses that even after a full blaze of his guns there are still huge piles of statistical munitions available to hand. He sets out the record with brutal clarity. Scotland has had a persistent tendency to under-perform UK growth. Between 1970 and 2000, Scottish GDP grew at an average of 1.8 per cent per annum while the UK grew at 2.2 per cent per annum. That is, the annual Scottish growth rate was 18 per cent lower than for the UK. Between 1997 and 2004, the absolute growth rate of Scottish GDP averaged 1.7 per cent while the UK average was 2.6 per cent. Even allowing for differences in statistical compilation and treatment, Scotland's growth rate is probably worse than before and the gap with the UK (notwithstanding a narrowing in 2005 as the UK economy slowed) has widened considerably. Manufacturing export sales have fallen every single quarter bar one since the end of 2000 and are now nearly 40 per cent less in real terms than they were five years ago. Scotland fares poorly in productivity comparisons and has run a persistent balance of payments deficit both with the UK and the rest of the world.

In his paper, **Professor Sir Donald MacKay,** a widely respected economist and former chairman of Scottish Enterprise, sets Scotland's performance and prospects in a global context. He shows that to share fully in the benefits of globalization any region needs a range of activities capable of

has taken is to transfer resources from the high to the low-productivity areas of the economy.

And not least, it sidesteps the very problem that Ward was seeking to bring to public attention: the inadequate rate of company formation in Scotland and how the business start-up rate continues to lag behind that of the UK as a whole.

Concerns expressed to the Scottish Parliament have also gone unheeded. For example, Wolfgang Michalski, an adviser to the Scottish Parliament's Business Growth Inquiry, set out this charge in a paper in the summer of 2005 to the economy committee:

Scotland's aggregate government expenditure corresponds to around 50 per cent of GDP and the net borrowing requirement above 10 per cent. It may be advisable for both to ensure that there is not a trend of a further increase in the longer-run.

More important, however, and perhaps even more worrying appears the composition of the expenditure. Taking identifiable expenditure on services by programme in 2002/03, 40 per cent of the Scottish budget is on social protection and nearly 20 per cent on health, whereas – apart from education and training with about 16 per cent – other potentially future orientated expenditures on services such as science and technology and enterprise and economic development combined reach no more than two per cent. In the same vein, two further questions arise: first, why are per capita expenditures for employment policies and for general public services in Scotland by and large twice as high as in the UK? And second, with a relation of about £38 million to £1.9 million in 2003, is there not a dramatic imbalance between public consumption and public investment? There may be good reasons for all this, but an outside observer could have some doubt whether

Scottish policies do not tend to subsidise the present at the expense of the future.[3]

Within the broader point he was making, Mr Michalski had picked up on telling statistics showing that while the First Minister continued to proclaim a rhetorical commitment to economic growth as 'the top priority', Scottish Executive primary expenditure on economic development between 1996–97 and 2005–06 has actually fallen, both in absolute terms and as a proportion of the spending total (from 7.8 per cent to 5.1 per cent). Even spending on roads, a key component of economic infrastructure, has barely risen over the past ten years.

Yet both this point and the greater points he made have remained unaddressed by the Executive in all its laboured attempts to gloss over the concerns about the high and rising level of public expenditure.

All this leaves an impression that devolution has turned into the story of the emperor's new clothes. It is government by vanity mirror. No blemishes can be seen in this hall of warped and flattering reflections. Instead, a relentless stream of new initiatives, strategies, targets and task forces is set up with almost every month in a whirlwind of activity and busyness while the work of previous initiatives and strategies and task forces has been ignored or forgotten, or not given the time and resources to complete. Obsessive busy-ness has come to be a substitute for results and the achievement of desired goals.

Devolution has not, as many had hoped, achieved 'breakout', but has, on the contrary, extended and magnified the worst features of a political culture of dependence that treats

---

3   Business Growth Inquiry. Paper by Wolfgang Michalski, adviser to the Committee EC/S2/05/16/5. Annex A, p. 6.

government as an auction of biddable benefits: 'free' care for the elderly; 'free' tuition fees; 'free' eye care, 'free' bridge tolls. There is not, and never has been, any such thing as a 'free' public good or benefit. But the pretence is maintained as it plays to the interest of the ruling coalition to sustain the pretence that its generosity is self-created and not dependent on funding arrangements agreed at Westminster. The truth is that this is not a parliament in the Westminster sense because it is not accountable to voters for the money it spends so liberally. The problem is that so long as the parliament can continue to disburse tax revenue without the need to raise taxation, voters cannot apply the sanction of choices on funding or spending. This is the profound disconnect at the heart of Scottish devolution, and it is one that will prove unsustainable.

Equally problematic have been attempts to raise our national confidence and self-esteem. This failure is particularly evident in the field of arts and cultural policy. Since devolution there has been a series of culture ministers, from Lord Watson to Frank McAveety, who seemed quite unsuited to their jobs and out of their depth. Scottish Opera hit a financial and management crisis resulting in the axing of its chorus and a year of silence. A succession of high-blown arts 'strategies' and initiatives has come and gone.

Of particular note was the depressing affair of the year-long Cultural Commission. Here an opportunity to lay down a clear statement of principles and priorities was lost in a document running to several hundred pages of impenetrable management-school verbiage, a list of more than a hundred unprioritized recommendations and a final publication that ran to fewer than a dozen printed copies as the money (stretching to more than £500,000) had run out. The entire exercise was both a deep disappointment to Scotland's rich artistic and creative talent and an object lesson in how not to go about policy formulation intended to clarify thinking and to present ministers with clear, particular, specific, achievable policy actions.

Sir Timothy Clifford, former head of the National Galleries of Scotland, publicly denounced the Commission's 'Soviet' approach to the arts and its centralizing proposals. Others boggled at some of its more vague and woolly recommendations, such as the creation of a 'National Creative Industries Sectoral Council' and a 'national strategy for story-telling'. Others feared it would trigger a headlong expansion in the arts bureaucracy.

Many were repelled by its bureaucratic gobbledygook, of which this sentence is typical: 'The process of rights and entitlements provides a starting point for the establishment of a framework of nationwide standards which should allow benchmarking to encourage providers to aim for above average results.' Said one baffled reader: 'Anyone who writes a sentence like that, particularly in a report on our national culture, should be taken out, put up against a wall, and shot.'

The Commission struggled under two misconceptions. The first was an approach that treated the arts as a part of manufacturing industry: every £100 of public money stuffed in would produce £100 of 'benchmarked' arts 'ingots' at the other end. In fact, the money is more likely to be absorbed in the implied huge increase in arts officials. Struggling arts organizations desperate for cash found little comfort.

The second was its failure to grasp a simple distinction: it is not the job of the Executive to 'manufacture arts'. It is to ensure there is a climate that allows artistic activity to flourish. How ironic that the report should have hailed the success of the Edinburgh Festival Fringe, which has the tiniest staff.

Morale in the arts community is now arguably lower than it was before the wretched Cultural Commission came into being. Little wonder that the composer James MacMillan blazed away in *The Sunday Times*:

Any objective observer of Holyrood sees a catalogue of immaturity, incompetence and a fundamental lack of political intelligence, writ large for the world to see . . . As an artist, the one issue I would dearly love to see being reserved back to Westminster is arts policy. It is in cultural matters that Holyrood seems most clueless and inept. It has had its chance and proved woefully lost and excruciatingly visionless . . . What baffles me about my fellow artists is that they can see this failure for themselves; they can see cultural policy is pathetically inferior to that south of the border, and yet they continue their craven support for proven philistines and enemies of serious culture who only do harm to Scotland's artistic reputation.[4]

*   *   *

Looking forward, how might positive change be effected? The book is divided into four sections: history and culture, the economy, politics and the constitution and society and welfare. The authors put forward a range of options and solutions for discussion.

It is appropriate the collection should open with an essay by the historian and author **Allan Massie**. He is sympathetic to the Scottish Parliament being given more powers to raise the money it spends. He believes electoral reform is essential, with an end to the List system and with all MSPs made directly responsive to voters. He would also like to see devolution of power and responsibility to local authorities. His conclusion is an elegantly put paradox: 'Only those committed to

---

4 Letter to *The Sunday Times*, 4 December 2005. MacMillan added for good measure: 'The Scottish parliament has proved incapable of doing the basics of governance: it has consistently squandered any claim or right to extending its powers; and there is a legitimate argument in proposing a curtailment of its activities.'

independence can be content to see things for the time being remain as they are. Those who were most strongly opposed to devolution now have the most cogent reason for trying to make it work effectively.'

On the economy, **George Kerevan** concludes that we should cease to support offshore manufacturing and encourage as much as possible of manufacture here. Positive steps could include promoting engineering education at secondary and graduate level, reviving inward investment strategies and funding showcase technology projects such as a bullet train between Glasgow and Edinburgh.

Professor Sir Donald MacKay argues that the best way to encourage the birth and development of new businesses is not through intervention by government agencies but a reduction in business taxes. A review of international evidence over almost three decades suggests that a reduction in business taxes of 10 per cent increases the annual growth rate of an economy by some two per cent.[5] Specifically he suggests a phased reduction of local business rates by 25 per cent a year over four years.

On politics and the constitution, **Gerald Warner** also proposes the abolition of List MSPs and a reduction in the number of members to around 106, in harmony with the recent cut in MPs. He advocates a revising chamber to moderate the more outrageous legislative initiatives of the parliament. 'Any Holyrood election with a turnout below 50 per cent', he declares, 'should be invalidated and re-run.' Reformers should also consider holding a second, confirmatory referendum on the existence of the parliament. An alternative reform is to make MSPs and MPs the same people, sitting at Holyrood three days a week and at Westminster on one day set aside for Scottish business on reserved matters. That would effectively remove a

---

5 *Journal of Public Economics*, June 2005.

superfluous tier of government and reduce the salary costs of members, besides finally resolving the West Lothian question.

Alan Cochrane, writing with formidable experience of Scottish politics, sets out well how devolution is fulfilling predictions both that it would create pressure for greater powers and that it would shoot the nationalist fox. He posits a party realignment, with the possibility of a Conservative–SNP axis. Formal partnership would be putting it too strongly, and the SNP leadership has moved quickly to dampen such talk. Nevertheless, Cochrane has detected a growing commonality of interest between some of the Conservative advocates of fiscal autonomy and elements in the SNP who fear the party has grown too close to the Far Left Scottish Socialist Party.

Tom Miers, writing from a libertarian perspective, warns against the 'tyranny of the majority' that inheres in a single chamber parliament and would like to see a second, revising chamber to avoid the legislative onslaught from narrow lobby groups and those pursuing sectional interests. **Brian Monteith**, the one MSP among the contributors, brings an insider's insight in his plea for greater scrutiny of parliamentary legislation. He, too, argues the case for a second chamber and that Scotland's various Czars for health, crime, food, drugs and alcohol should be required to report direct to parliament.

On social issues and welfare, **Fraser Nelson** argues that we need to crack the dependency culture by making Scotland a test case for American-style welfare reform. Incapacity benefit claimants must be reassessed: those able to work should be required to do so. Control of schools and hospitals must be taken from the Scottish bureaucratic class and handed to the professionals. This can be done by a choice agenda described (but not implemented) by Mr Blair in England.

On health reform, **Gillian Bowditch** puts the case for NHS Scotland to follow the English model and become more efficient. 'This is one case', she argues, 'where we should acknowledge that what are needed are English solutions for Scottish problems.'

Experience tells us not that change is impossible but that the longer it is delayed the more costly and convulsive it is likely to be. It is this freedom to change, not the forces arrayed in defence of the prevailing order, that history has shown to have the greater power.

Scots over the centuries have come to value their freedom greatly. Today that freedom has never been more potent. Not just the strength, but the survival of a free people flows, as it historically has always flowed, from the freedom to make choices and the freedom to change.

To despair is a sin. We should never succumb to the doctrine of 'this is how it has to be'. Quite the opposite is true. Here are ten reasons why.

*　　　　*　　　　*

Bill Jamieson is Executive Editor of *The Scotsman,* economics columnist for *The Business* and Director of the Policy Institute. Previous books include *Britain Beyond Europe* (Duckworth, 1995); *An Illustrated Guide to the British Economy* (Duckworth, 1998) and *An Illustrated Guide to the Scottish Economy,* ed. (Duckworth, 1999). He lives in Edinburgh.

Spending and taxation in Scotland

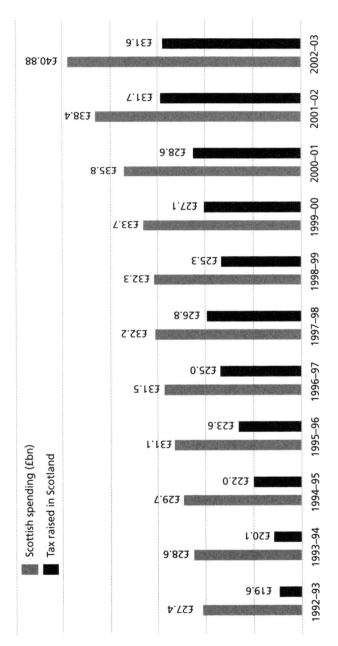

Scottish spending (£bn)

Tax raised in Scotland

Year	Scottish spending (£bn)	Tax raised in Scotland
1992–93	£27.4	£19.6
1993–94	£28.6	£20.1
1994–95	£29.7	£22.0
1995–96	£31.1	£23.6
1996–97	£31.5	£25.0
1997–98	£32.2	£26.8
1998–99	£32.3	£25.3
1999–00	£33.7	£27.1
2000–01	£35.8	£28.6
2001–02	£38.4	£31.7
2002–03	£40.88	£31.6

Source: Scotland Office: *Government Expenditure & Revenue in Scotland*

Scotland's contribution to UK economy

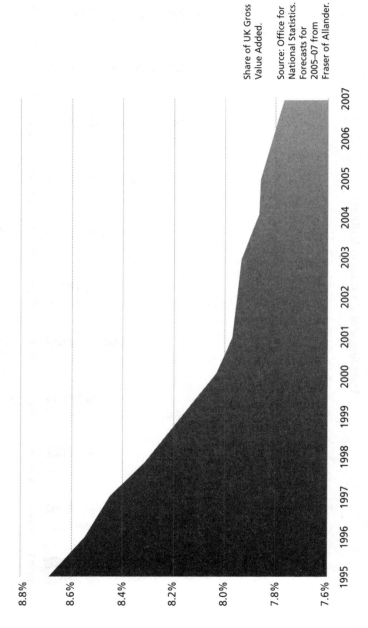

Share of UK Gross
Value Added.

Source: Office for
National Statistics.
Forecasts for
2005–07 from
Fraser of Allander.

History and Culture

ALLAN MASSIE

1

Change is the best option
for the status quo

TOWARDS THE END OF the last century I was asked to write a book about Anglo–Scottish relations. The proposal came from a Scottish editor in a London publishing house, itself, in the long distant past, a Scottish foundation. She had in mind that the book, while not a work of propaganda, should be written from a Unionist point of view.

It was a long time in the writing, and I often came close to abandoning it, only financial necessity keeping me going. It seemed that everything interesting on the subject had already been said, too frequently. Moreover, when devolution became unavoidable after the Referendum of September 1997, the book's relevance was diminished. Theoretically of course the continuation of the Union remained a political issue, while the Scottish National Party, committed to the abrogation of the Treaty of 1707, was the principal opposition grouping in the new parliament.

But the steam had gone out of that debate. Scotland was settling into a half-way house, or quarter or three-quarter way, whichever you prefer. The reality of the parliament disappointed many who had hoped for great things and who had talked enthusiastically of the vibrant and vigorously creative New Scotland that would emerge. In October 2005 the

novelist William McIlvanney remarked in an interview: 'I
sense a recession in the strength of Scottishness almost just by
having the parliament'. Of course six years is a very short
time in the life of a nation. Nevertheless, for the time being
political argument has subsided, enthusiasm for further constitutional change is not evident, but has been replaced by a
settled apathy.

Despite everything, the book was finished and was published in the summer of 2005 with the title *The Thistle and
the Rose,* which, though neither striking nor original, was at
least self-explanatory. By this time the editor who commis-
sioned it had moved on, as editors tend to do in the publishing business now; and, though she had shown exemplary
patience as I missed delivery date after delivery date, this may
have been just as well. For I doubt if the book was quite what
she had wanted. It certainly made no cogent case for the
political Union. Indeed, in the conclusion to what was, to me,
a surprisingly laudatory review, Irvine Welsh (author of
Trainspotting, no less) wrote: 'Strangely, Massie the unionist
offers at least as much succour to the nationalist cause. Hume
would be proud of such scepticism; how much more Scottish
can you get?'

This was pleasing; no one after all can fail to find a supposed
resemblance to Hume anything but flattering. But setting that
aside, I suspect Welsh's judgement may be accurate. Perhaps,
as Blake said of Milton, I was 'of the Devil's party without
knowing it'.

My publisher gave it the sub-title 'Six Centuries of Love and
Hate between the Scots and the English'. This, if not an accurate description of the content, was at least eye-catching. But
several reviewers observed, sensibly, that the words 'love and
hate' were far too strong. 'Friendship', 'affection', 'irritation',
'boredom', 'misunderstandings' might all have been more to
the point, though duller and therefore less marketable.

Instead of an argument pursued to a conclusion, the book seems, to me anyway, to have turned out to be a meditation: on the resemblance and differences, the two-way influences, the bonds and divisions, as they have emerged across the centuries. And perhaps this is appropriate. Perhaps it strikes the right note. Perhaps meditation – a period of contemplation – is what is needed now.

That meditation must start with the word 'British'. We all use it. Everyone with a passport will find himself described as a 'British citizen'. We talk comfortably about 'the British Empire', 'the British war effort of 1939–45', 'the British army', 'the British Olympic team'. We may talk about 'the British character'. Even Scottish Nationalists admit, if reluctantly, the existence of some sort of British identity. This is implicit in the assurance given by Alex Salmond that what he calls 'the social union' would survive the breaking of the United Kingdom; for what is this social union if it is not British?

Yet three centuries of political union have not supplied us with a satisfactory noun. George III may have gloried in 'the name of Britain', but nobody identifies himself as 'a Briton' as he might say 'I'm a Scot', or 'I'm an Englishman'. Expatriates may call themselves 'Brits' and the word has been taken up by the tabloid press, but few of us use it comfortably. When spoken, the word is usually supplied with silent inverted commas. 'British' may be an overarching identity, but within that arch, the older national distinctions persist.

The contrast with Germany and the Germans is instructive. Germany's history as a unified nation-state is much shorter than the history of the United Kingdom, dating only from 1871. That German union has subsequently been interrupted (1945–91) while the boundaries of the state have shifted and contracted. Yet German identity, based on the idea of the German Volk, transcends all. There is no British Volk.

Volkisch identities within the United Kingdom are English, Scots, Irish and Welsh, their persistence remarkable and undeniable. At the end of the nineteenth century the French political scientist Emile Boutmy found that 'the so-called United Kingdom was made up of four nations in a condition of permanent irritation with each other'. This is still the case.

Yet these nations have been changed by the experience of union. They are what they are today as a result of that political fact, the United Kingdom. The Anglicization of Scotland is evident; our language is English, not Scots or Gaelic. That English may be spoken with a Scots accent and even with an admixture of old (and new) Scots words, but essentially it differs little, if any, more from standard English than does the English spoken in Newcastle, Liverpool or Leeds.

The Scottish influence on England and English culture may be less immediately apparent. It is nevertheless no less profound. For centuries England has been open to immigration from Scotland, and much that now seems English, even characteristically English, is the result of that immigration. Scots have been responsible for the making of institutions such as the Oxford English Dictionary, the Dictionary of National Biography and the Encyclopaedia Britannica. They have shaped economic and social policy. Margaret Thatcher believed herself to be a disciple of Adam Smith – a claim also made by the younger Pitt – and could not for this reason understand why her policies met with such fierce resistance in Scotland.

Again, it was Scots – Hume in the eighteenth century, Macaulay in the nineteenth – who taught the English their own history, and helped form their idea of the sort of people they were, while, in *Ivanhoe*, Walter Scott gave the English a sense of their mediaeval past, elaborating the myth of 'Merrie England'. In the twentieth century that most British of institutions, the BBC, took its tone, temper and ethos from the

son of a Scots manse, John Reith, while the influence of
Scotch journalists on the interpretation of public events has
been, and remains, considerable.

The examples could be offered, at great length. It's enough
here to remark that while opponents of devolution in the
1970s campaigned on the slogan 'Scotland is British', a statement then of fact as well as opinion, it would be at least
equally true to assert that 'Britain is Scottish'.

Nevertheless it is undeniable that, within Scotland, the
sense of Britishness has weakened over the last half-century.
This is so well recognized that it is unnecessary to do more
than point very briefly to some reasons: the dissolution of the
Empire, the centralization of the state and the consequent
dominance of Westminster and Whitehall, the moral effect
of the United Kingdom's loss of the status of a Great Power.
The result has been resurgent nationalism and political
devolution.

A note on that nationalist resurgence is desirable. It has been
provoked not by a widening difference between Scotland and
England, but by the erosion of differences, the disappearance
of distinctions. For the first two centuries of political union,
religion marked one such distinction. Scotland was Presbyterian, and, though Scots Presbyterianism had much in common
with English Dissent or Nonconformity, nevertheless, the
established Church of England was very different from the
Scots Kirk.

Stevenson drew attention to the difference between them
in an essay entitled 'The Foreigner at Home'. 'The whole of
the two divergent systems', he wrote, 'is summed up, not
speciously, in the first two questions of the rival catechisms,
the English tritely enquiring, "What is your name?", the Scottish striking at the very roots of life with "What is the chief
end of Man?" and answering nobly, if obscurely, "to glorify
God and to enjoy Him for ever".' Consequently, he thought

'about the very cradle of the Scot there goes a hum of metaphysical divinity'. That hum is silent now, and such Christianity as survives in Scotland is like that surviving in England: tepid, unassertive, more concerned with 'social justice' than with metaphysics.

Scottish cultural nationalism, renascent in the second half of the twentieth century, was fostered less by an apprehension of our difference from England than by the fear that differences and distinction were disappearing, and must therefore be reasserted. And it was this cultural nationalism, rather than questions of utility, which inspired the political demand for Home Rule or Independence.

As a journalist, I argued against devolution, persistently right up to the referendum of September 1997, and with such cogency as I could muster. I did so for two reasons. First, I still felt British and it seemed probable that any scheme of devolution would lead eventually to separation. Second, the argument for devolution was founded in dishonesty, and the powers proposed for the parliament seemed risibly inadequate, so much so indeed as to compound the dishonesty.

It was maintained that Scotland suffered a 'democratic deficit': Scotland voted Labour and got a Tory government. This of course was true, but devolution could not correct that deficit. It was indeed an argument for independence, not devolution. On the eve of the referendum, I wrote: 'Set up a Scottish parliament as proposed in the White Paper and then look at the list of powers reserved to Westminster. You will see that next time we have a Westminster government which does not command majority support in Scotland, it will still take decisions on a wide range of affairs which concern us; and these decisions will affect us and the way we live just as surely as if there was no Scottish parliament or its members had been banished to St Kilda.'

As for that parliament it seemed to me to be a mere parody

of a parliament, one with small powers and little responsibility. It offered very limited Home Rule, restricted almost entirely to those areas of government which had already been administratively devolved to the Scottish Office.

Moreover, and most damagingly, the financial provisions for the parliament appeared to me ridiculous. 'It is not healthy', I wrote, 'for a supposedly responsible body to be so dependent on another superior body for its revenue.'

In support of this argument I quoted another *Scotsman* journalist, Iain MacWhirter, then a cheerleader for devolution. Writing about the malaise of local government, he had said: 'Part of the problem is that local councils no longer raise the money they spend. Nothing could be better calculated to undermine civic responsibility. The balance should be restored with more tax raised locally and less raised centrally. Councils would then be answerable to their local electorate . . .'

Nothing could be better calculated to undermine civic responsibility. . . . Yet a parliament was being proposed that would have even less responsibility for raising its revenue than the meanest local authority in the land. The parliament and executive would enjoy all the pleasure of spending money without incurring the odium of raising it. This did not appear to be a recipe for good government.

I had other, though lesser, reasons for being opposed to devolution. We were promised a new style of politics, and I did not think this likely. The idea that talented people who had fought shy of political involvement would now seek membership of the new parliament seemed to me fanciful, and has since proved unfounded.

Moreover, I could not believe that many of the more able Scottish MPs would desert Westminster for the Scottish Parliament, and this too has proved to be the case, the likes of Gordon Brown, John Reid, George Robertson, the late Robin Cook and Charles Kennedy all choosing to remain members of the House of Commons, to which body even the SNP leader Alex Salmond opted to return in 2001.

Now, more than six years into the new regime, and with the third Scottish parliamentary election looming on the horizon, disillusion is undeniable. It is indeed most evident among many who were the most enthusiastic advocates for devolution. It is quite common to hear journalists who campaigned for the parliament describe its members as 'numpties', and the body itself as the 'numptorium'. Disappointed or cheated lovers are ever the most bitter.

Those of us in the other camp at the time of the referendum may be more relaxed. Certainly the thing has turned out to be no better than we expected, but then it is no worse either. We thought it would achieve little of value; and it hasn't. We doubted whether it would improve the quality of government in Scotland, and our doubts have been justified. We said it would be a parody of a parliament, and this is what is has shown itself to be.

Only in one respect have our fears proved unfounded – so far at least. There is no evidence that the existence of the parliament has stimulated desire for independence; indeed, as already suggested, it may even for the time being have damped down any demand that the Union should be broken.

If so, then, one of Labour's aims in espousing devolution may seem to have been achieved. The SNP is becalmed, drifting in the doldrums. Stopping the SNP was the aim of Labour's first attempt at devolution in the 1970s. By 1997 there was another aim, more urgent for Labour. This was to resist change such as Margaret Thatcher had imposed on the United Kingdom by means of her majority in England. Thus regarded, Labour's purpose was essentially conservative. As the young nobleman Tancredi says in Lampedusa's novel *The Leopard*, 'things will have to change if we want them to remain the same'.

And this is what has happened since 1999. The change which gave us the Scottish Parliament has enabled the Scottish Labour Party to avoid making the public service reforms which Tony Blair has been attempting in England. Devolution, Labour's answer to Thatcherism, has turned out to be the means of checking Blairism. It has allowed Scotland to withdraw behind a defensive laager, self-absorbed, parochial and myopic.

This is profoundly unsatisfactory. Far from being a stimulant, devolution has proved soporific. The New Scotland we were promised proves a mirage, dissolving before our eyes. Instead we have the old statist Scotland, averse to innovation, suspicious of enterprise, dominated by an over-heavy public sector.

So what's to be done?

The starting-point must be the acceptance that the Scotland Act will not be repealed, the Parliament and Executive will not disappear. Devolution is a reality that is here to stay. To dream or pretend otherwise is sheer Jacobitism: emotionally satisfying, practically pointless.

It is to the credit of the Scottish Tory Party that it has accepted this reality, though it opposed devolution to the last ditch. But, though it has accepted the reality, it has not yet embraced it. It has not yet addressed itself to the question: how do we make this unwanted parliament function effectively?

Three things seem necessary. All demand an act of faith, difficult as this must be for those who distrusted the enterprise from the start.

First, the Parliament must be made to assume real responsibility for what it does. This means that it must raise the money it spends. You cannot have good government without fiscal responsibility, fiscal autonomy. Some who assent to the theory shrink from the practice. They do not think our politicians can be trusted. They point to the large number of Scots who do not pay income tax, and who will therefore always vote for a party that promises higher public spending, since they will not have to pay for it. They point to the army of public sector workers likely to be compensated for tax rises by salary and age increases. These objections are not contemptible. The fear that Scots will not vote for a party promising lower taxes has some foundation. There is however one possible remedy. The Scottish Parliament should be made responsible for imposing income tax, but the system known as PAYE which renders payment of income tax comparatively painless for all employees should be abolished. People in general pay more in income tax than in council tax, but the latter is far more unpopular, because it is paid directly from money already in the taxpayer's possession. If it is desirable to make parliament responsible, it is no less desirable to instil the same sense of responsibility in voters. Abolishing PAYE would have that effect. It would make the link between tax-paying and public expenditure transparent.

Second, electoral reform is essential. The existence of List MSPs responsible to their party rather than to the electorate is absurd and indefensible. All MSPs should be directly responsive to voters, not to their party chiefs. Since we have multi-party politics, the first-past-the-post electoral system cannot give a satisfactory result; it is suited only to a two-party state. Election to the parliament should be by the single transferable vote in multi-member constituencies. This allows the electorate to dismiss unsatisfactory members.

Third, there has to be a real devolution of power and responsibility to local authorities. This proposal too is unlikely to be popular, because local authorities are held in low esteem. Nevertheless, it's necessary. Local authorities are at present mere instruments of the centralized state, satellites without autonomy. They, too, should be required to raise most of what they spend.

One way to make this possible would be to allow councils to retain a share of VAT paid by businesses within their local authority area. Nothing could be better calculated to have them eager to encourage business and enterprise.

The changes proposed may all be described as structural, aimed at making the political system work more effectively to the general good. They stand in a different order from matters of policy affecting, for instance, the health service, schools and universities. Objections may be raised to all of them, but they have this in common, this to commend them: enacting these reforms would make for more responsible government; and it is responsibility which is now lacking.

Devolution represents a middle way between the unitary state we knew until 1999, and independence. So far our experience of this middle way has been unhappy, disappointing to many who urged it on us, rendering cynical many who opposed it. Since we are not going to revert to the unitary state, it behoves all who regard themselves as both Scots and British to devise a means of making that middle way function effectively.

If it continues as it is – irresponsible, unimaginative, feeble, and yet self-satisfied – then there will some day be no option but to break the link with the other parts of the United Kingdom and launch ourselves on the uncertain sea of independence.

The truth is this: only those who are committed to independence can be content to see things for the time being continue as they are. Those who were more strongly opposed to devolution now have the most cogent reason for trying to make it work effectively.

*   *   *

Allan Massie is a journalist and one of Scotland's most respected authors. Books include *Change and Decay in All Around I See*; *The Last Peacock*; *The Death of Men* (Scottish Arts Council Book Award); *One Night in Winter*; *Shadows of Empire*; *A Question of Loyalties* and *The Sins of the Father*. Non-fiction works include *The Caesars* and *Great Scots*. His latest book *The Thistle and The Rose* was published in 2005. He lives in Selkirk.

MICHAEL FRY

2

Scotland the victim-nation

THERE ARE NOT MANY COUNTRIES in the world where the past proclaims itself as powerfully as in Scotland. In Edinburgh people still tread the very streets that David Hume or Adam Smith or Sir Walter Scott trod. Certain parts of Glasgow may recall the model modern metropolis which the Victorian city fathers sought to build.

Smaller towns are better still: on Cromarty or Kelso, on Inveraray or Inverbervie, some previous age has often set its stamp and left them as gems after their own kind, full of charm and individuality.

And that is not even to speak of more evocative reminders of our past, at Iona where Dr Samuel Johnson felt his piety warmed on behalf of all mankind, at Traprain Law where Richard Wagner's hero Tristan came from, at Callanish where the first natives of Scotland cultivated not only their crops but also a spiritual harmony with the inclement seasons.

So Scotland is a country on which a turbulent history is impressed ineffaceably and where by tradition most of the people have felt that history, for all its dark drama, to be something of which they can feel proud.

Certainly that was true of previous generations. We see that from the statues erected all over the country, the thickest clusters round George Square in Glasgow and along Princes Street in Edinburgh, to all the great Scots. In these memorials a martial *motif* figures with special prominence, and there cannot be a town or village in the country lacking a monument to the glorious dead in every war of the twentieth century.

They are particularly poignant when, on Skye or Shetland, they stand by a still loch or an empty glen, where hardly anyone remains to remember. Yet the tradition continues. It seemed to the nation natural to commemorate the late Donald Dewar with a statue, the character of the man mirrored in an eccentric design and the slightly bizarre life after death it has led.

But lately the Scots' traditional pride in their history has turned sour. As the historian of *The Scottish Empire,* I have noted it especially in that whole side of the narrative of the nation, what we might call its external history, which in modern times has been somewhat more uplifting than the bleak internal history. The Empire was indeed after 1707 the arena where Scots showed their finest qualities, though sometimes also their basest, fuelled by the energies released after they ceased to be confined within the bounds of their own small country.

For generations, Scots vaunted themselves on the achievements that followed – everything from the Canadian Pacific Railway to the evangelization of Africa, to the jute industry of Bengal, to the very existence of the modern city-states of Hong Kong and Singapore. Some of the record was again dark, as the record of all great human endeavours is in part dark. But the light diffused by it far outshone the dark.

For a nation of its size, everyone used to agree, Scotland's contribution to the progress and welfare of mankind was astonishing. Like it or not, the Empire was the main channel through which Scottish qualities of mind and character have flowed out all over the world.

Like it or not, I have to say, for nowadays there are many

people who do not like it. They have come to the view that this imperial record is, on the contrary, something of which Scots ought to be ashamed. The critics of imperialism prefer to denigrate all those endless achievements in Africa or America or Asia. Even a great explorer such as David Livingstone, who mapped the interior of a continent and showed its relation to the outside world, is said to have discovered nothing because the territory he traversed was already known to its inhabitants. It is fortunate that at least the Africans still revere him as a man who truly loved their lands and peoples, where the Scots of today no longer care to.

By the same token, those who followed him into the heart of darkness and tried to introduce some form of economic life other than the slave trade are condemned as exploiters – as if exploitation of natural resources were not morally superior to exploitation of human beings.

Post-imperial guilt ensures the triumph of such criticism all over the Western world. Even in Scotland, which gave so much to the Empire and took so much from it, the Scots' imperial role is now commonly regarded as a matter for remorse. So far as children in our schools are today taught anything about Empire, they are taught that it was nothing to be proud of.

They will then be taught nothing about Scots fulfilling themselves by fulfilling a role in the wider world, as colonial governors or Presbyterian missionaries or the architects and engineers who built dams, bridges, railways, harbours and so on *ad infinitum*. If our schools do impart anything about Empire on a human level, it will be about those Scots supposed to have lived on the same level and in the same predicament as the native peoples in exotic climes. As I write I have in front of me a recent book aimed at primary pupils, *Children of the Clearances*, written by David Ross and published by Waverley Books of New Lanark. It begins:

My name is Jessie. I am going to tell you about some of the things that happened in Scotland during a time in our history called the Clearances. In the Highlands and Islands, many Scottish clansmen and their families were forced to leave their homes during the Clearances. They were living on small farms but men who owned the land wanted to set up huge sheep farms. They believed the only way to do this was to drive the ordinary people away. And so it was that the poor people, like my family, lost not only their belongings and their homes but their whole way of life. Many were forced to leave Scotland for ever to seek a new life in the colonies.

There the link between exploitation at home and abroad becomes specific, joining the fates of Highlanders and of natives in distant continents.

It is interesting, however, that Waverley Books of New Lanark has, to my knowledge, published nothing on that former ideal community where it has set up in business, run two centuries ago by Robert Owen with a view to making human beings as efficient as machines. He asked fellow employers: 'Now, if the care which you bestow upon machinery can give you such excellent results, may you not expect equally good results from care spent upon human beings, with their infinitely superior structure?'

But then Owen is counted as a forerunner of socialism, so obviously his own exploitation of workers leaves him free of any moral taint. Readers might, however, like to seek out what he had to say about black people when he went to set up a similar ideal community on the banks of Wabash River in the United States. His remarks would certainly not pass the test of political correctness today.

The trouble is that Scots have come to prefer a history replete with caricatures rather than with real human beings who were a mixture of flesh and blood, of good and bad, of virtue and vice. What else can we expect of a nation where the Minister of Education, Peter Peacock, suggests the study of history in schools might be given up? The life of the past could be – Heavens above! – just as complex and ambiguous as the life of the present. Perhaps it would be nicer if we did not have to deal with the rich, deep, complex motivation actually driving humanity, of which history offers us examples we can analyse and appreciate the better because we view them with some detachment. Far better, no doubt, for us to be assigned pre-ordained roles by our political masters without having to think for ourselves.

The role that seems to have been chosen for Scots, and so far happily accepted by them, is the role of victims. It instils a conviction useful to politicians, that the rest of the world owes the victims a living. For this, see more or less any debate in the Scottish Parliament, but one dealing with public expenditure especially. Add to the mixture the idea that money grows on trees, and that the victim has no responsibility for raising the sum to be spent on him – and we have a perfect picture of the Scottish political system as we advance into the twenty-first century.

This development would have astonished previous generations of Scots. One hundred years ago they had just entered the twentieth century with an exceedingly good conceit of themselves. Evidence was compiled in 1894–5 by Lord Rosebery's Liberal government which actually showed Scotland to be the richest of the four nations in the United Kingdom. The figures were generated as a financial touchstone for the debate at the time on Home Rule all round, or devolution as we now call it. They may not have attained the standards of statistical rigour that would be required of such an exercise today. But they underlined that Scotland was doing well, and probably better than the rest of Britain.

That phase of high Victorian prosperity had gone on since the onset of the second stage of the Industrial Revolution about 1870, with a shift towards the heavy end of production – coal, steel and shipbuilding – in which Scotland could specialize. Clyde-built vessels sailed the seven seas, made of Scottish plates and joist, burning Scottish coal. They linked an Empire on which the sun never set.

They also made up most of the merchants or naval fleets in such unlikely foreign lands as Chile, Turkey or Japan. Glasgow, lying at the centre of this complex of production, was an opulent city-state undertaking extravagant investment to offer its citizens a range of facilities, from art galleries to telephones to medical services, later thought to be the province of national rather than merely municipal government. It is true Glaswegians were badly housed and not in good health. Still, they felt superior, not only to the citizens of Edinburgh, needless to say, but also to those of London.

One key to the character of Victorian Scots was their stupendous confidence in themselves and what they set out to achieve. In 1855 a migrant Scotsman from Haddington called Samuel Smiles published in London a book called *Self-Help*. It brought him fame and fortune. To contemporaries it showed the way forward in life for any man, or woman, who lacked the money or connections of the aristocracy. This way forward for the great majority, not a privileged minority, led directly out of the Scottish background in which Smiles had been brought up and the sterling human qualities with which it endowed him. People attributed these to Scottish religion or to Scottish education, or the hardiness induced by the climate and eating porridge for breakfast.

Whatever it was – and no two Scots would ever agree – it was reckoned to give them a sturdy sense of independence which, at the political level, spurned intervention by the state in industry and generally in civil society. As socialism emerged in England, among petal-sniffing aesthetes such as William Morris or humourless blue-stockings such as Beatrice Webb, the average red-blooded Scotsman was left cold. Up to the First World War, Glasgow looked down on London as a hotbed of social unrest, with managers who could not manage and workers who would not work. The sense of worth all round Scotland, not just in her largest city, was underpinned not only by industrial but also by scientific and artistic achievement which we may look back on in envy today. Scots felt they could do more or less anything, and they did.

In sum, Scotland had a culture owed to the victors in life-struggles. Scots came out almost everywhere on top. Scottish ships and railway-engines were the best in the world, as anyone could see by going to watch them at work not only in Britain but also in the Americas, Africa and Asia. Scottish scientists and engineers were the best in the world too – obviously, because they were the men who made the technological achievements possible. Scottish schools and universities were the best in the world as well, at least in educating the people rather than the elite that other nations privileged.

Such accomplished sons of the nation were spreading enlightenment round the globe, and by the mid-twentieth century could number in their ranks eight Nobel Prize winners, more per head than any other people on earth. Scottish workers were the best in the world, in high demand wherever the most advanced skills were needed, from San Francisco to Sydney. A Scot, Andrew Carnegie, was the richest man in the world, at least till he started giving his money away to a host of philanthropic projects, many of which survive to this day.

Whether or not Scotland remained the richest country in the world, could there be any doubt that she was the best country in the world?

And in those days, it was the character of the nation that

gave shape to its public life, not the other way round. Individual excellence as a product of individualism found expression in Scottish politics, not least in the four Prime Ministers during the decades on either side of the turn of the twentieth century: Lord Rosebery, A. J. Balfour, Henry Campbell-Bannerman and Andrew Bonar Law.

Nobody controlled the constituencies, and it was normal for different factions of national parties to fight one another there at the local level. No mechanism existed by which a central organization in Edinburgh, let alone London, could control them. Similarly, public policy rejected all local intervention by national government, including expenditure that could not be strictly covered by taxation.

The system was geared to citizens who worked for themselves, skilled craftsmen or small farmers – even the crofters elected men of their own choosing to Parliament, which they have never done since. Scots hated anything big, whether big estates and the lairds who owned them, or big government and the orders it sent down from London.

If we go on half a century to 1950 we find a Scotland transformed, and altogether for the bad. The most obvious difference from 1900 arose out of economic decline in the intervening period, which had robbed the west of Scotland especially of its prosperity.

That decline had first set in after the First World War, when Clydeside's former international markets shrank and never recovered. Glasgow turned into a slum. The middle class fled beyond the city's boundaries, leaving an inadequate tax-base for almost the sole new construction allowed by the council, of inferior public housing. Social conditions were the worst in Britain. The people grew poor, with only emigration as a refuge from unemployment. Not only the west but Scotland as a whole, from being a heavy outward investor, became a supplicant for inward investment. Indigenous ownership of industry shrank, leaving a branch economy for multinational corporations with headquarters abroad. After the slump of the 1930s came a brief boom during the Second World War. But when peace returned the mines faced closure, the steelworks would be next to go and already the shipbuilding industry was reduced to a shadow of its former self. That Scotland might have done better is demonstrated by the fact that other parts of Britain did, despite facing just the same problems. Whereas they gave themselves new economies, Scotland did not. Why not?

Perhaps the biggest transformation of all lay in the sense of grievance that Scotland had given herself. It was no longer a nation of victors but a nation of victims. In the course of the twentieth century victimhood became an industry with a rate of growth as good as coal or steel or shipbuilding had ever shown. And its cultural effect was greater than any other force in the nation's recent history. That history has today been rewritten to reinforce a sense of grievance. The history of Clydeside, in large part a history of independent craftsmen spurning socialism, has been turned into a history of capitalist exploitation, culminating in the abandonment of the region by the global economy.

The history of the Highlands, in large part the history of a culture's survival against stupendous odds, and the success of the people who with it equipped themselves to leave their native glens and successfully found new societies elsewhere, had been turned into a tale of relentless oppression and unrelieved suffering.

We could find further examples all the way back to the Wars of Independence in the fourteenth century, where nowadays King Robert Bruce, who actually won them, takes a back-seat to William Wallace, who did little more than get himself heroically hanged, drawn and quartered by the English.

The new Scotland, the Scotland of the twenty-first century,

is becoming a nation founded on grievance, real or imagined. Opening old wounds has become a national preoccupation. Under the Scottish Parliament, the nation is in danger of setting itself up as a refuge for all the lost causes of the previous century, socialism prominent among them. Blaming the English, too, for the country's troubles is one of the foundations of modern Scottish culture.

So now we have a culture not of victors but of victims. The economic problems of mid-century have been to quite a large extent overcome, and perhaps were never as bad as Scots imagined once they had made up their minds to do something about them rather than to wallow in them. Even so, a psychological effect remains. Scots still prefer to think of themselves as victims, even though chances to become victors again are there.

For example, Scotland reckons herself to be a poor country in constant need of aid or investment from the rest of Britain and overseas. In fact, in terms of GDP per head, she still ranks among the top 20 richest countries in the world. Scotland may no longer be among the leaders. But in real terms she is still five or six times wealthier than she was in 1900. Except for a break, no doubt, due to depression and war, Scots have seen a steady improvement in their living standards, so that death and disease are for most of us no longer due to deprivation but to an excess of the good things of life.

Scotland has fallen behind only because she has not continued to get rich as fast as other countries, England being the nearest and most galling example, Ireland the most recent and striking one, after she turned to capitalism from several decades of failed attempts to promote peasant agriculture. It may be noted that the promotion of peasant agriculture is one object of the Scottish Executive's land reforms. It is typical of the way we fall behind when do not have to.

We largely take for granted that only the state can direct and develop the Scottish economy. Yet every enterprise favoured by the state in the last few decades, from Govan Shipbuilders to the Invergordon smelter, has collapsed and disappeared. The industries that have survived and flourished, such as North Sea oil and the financial sector, have owed nothing whatever to the state. Indeed they have flourished despite disfavour from the state in the shape of penal taxation, respectively the Petroleum Revenue Tax and the Selective Employment Tax, a short-lived brainwave of Harold Wilson which sought to shift workers from services to manufactures – in precisely the opposite direction to the actual flow, at that time and now.

Some recent figures have shown that in many districts of Scotland the bulk of income arises from the state rather than from private enterprise: East Ayrshire headed the list at 70 per cent of income. Yet these places dependent on the state are the poorest, not the richest, in Scotland. The richest are those few places, such as Edinburgh and Aberdeen, where private enterprise still flourishes.

Why can't we see what has worked and what does work, what has not worked and what does not work, in the Scottish economy or in Scottish society more widely? Usually such blind spots are psychological rather than physiological. People do not see what is staring them in the face because they do not want to see it. It seems to me that Scots have come to prefer nursing their sense of grievance to taking realistic stock of their situation. If they did ever choose the latter option, they might even be inspired to do something about their situation. But Scots apparently prefer to presume that this is all somebody else's responsibility. If you have a sense of grievance, it is all too easy to conclude that the rest of the world owes you a living.

Scotland has today forgotten that she was ever a victor nation, able to do anything for herself. Now she is a victim nation, able to do nothing for herself, and needing the English or the Europeans or the Americans to do things for her. Yet perhaps the lessons of history show us that this need not be so.

The only new element is the existence of a Scottish Executive chanting a mantra that this is *Smart, Successful Scotland*: itself a notable case of self-delusion when the reality is of a dim, declining Scotland, going faster downhill since devolution came. The only good thing about the devolutionary settlement is that it might offer instruments to turn this Scotland round if we wanted to. The key, however, lies in the will to do it, not in persuading other people to give us the money to do it. Scotland began her long industrial ascent in the nineteenth century from a base of pitiful poverty.

What changed was not money from England, which never arrived till the industrial descent began, but the mentality of the people, with the drive to self-improvement and the sturdy desire for independence not only in the individual but in society as a whole.

My wish for 2020 is that something of that spirit can be reborn. But I will not hold my breath.

*   *   *

Michael Fry is a historian, economist and political commentator. His books include *The Scottish Empire* and *Wild Scots: Four Hundred Years of Highland History*. He lives in Edinburgh.

Economy

GEORGE KEREVAN

3

Devolution: A deepening economic policy failure

IN FEBRUARY 2003, in the run up to the second Holyrood election, the First Minister, Mr Jack McConnell, announced that improving Scotland's economic growth was to be his major priority:

> We are clear that getting Scotland's economy growing again is the most important thing we can do. Not for the sake of it, not so that our GDP statistics look good on paper, but for the long-term good of Scotland.

The First Minister has made improving Scotland's economic performance radically the signal test of devolution. Has he succeeded? What impact has the devolution settlement of 1999 had on the Scottish economy – good, bad or indifferent?

This chapter will do four things. First we will examine the raw data on economic performance since the devolved Scottish Parliament and Executive was established in 1999. Second, we will analyse the impact of the unprecedented expansion of public expenditure and state employment in Scotland post devolution with a view to understanding its implications for economic performance. Third, we will review and criticize the Executive's approach to economic policy. Fourth and last, we will lay out some policy conclusions.

1. Economic performance since 1999

a) GDP performance

Scotland has a persistent tendency to under-perform UK GDP growth. Between 1970 and 2000, Scottish GDP grew at an average of 1.8 per cent per annum, while the UK grew at 2.2 per cent per annum. That is, the annual Scottish growth rate was 18 per cent lower than for the UK. This long-term under-performance is the key feature of the Scottish economy. How has devolution affected this position?

Evidence: The absolute growth rate of Scottish GDP averaged 1.7 per cent per annum between 1999 and 2004 while the UK average was 2.6 per cent. There are differences in the methods of data collection and collation of GDP between Scotland and the rest of the UK that qualify such comparisons. But the orders of magnitude here are convincing. Since devolution, Scotland's growth rate is probably worse than before (though maybe not so different from the 1990s). On the other hand, the gap with the UK has widened considerably by any measure. On these figures, the gap has increased to 35 per cent.

Verdict: Devolution so far has not altered Scotland's poor trend rate of growth.

Note: The time period involved is probably too short for a final verdict, though devolution has been with us over one complete economic cycle which should be enough to identify trends. These growth figures also disguise a seismic shift in the economy – the collapse of hi-tech manufacturing output between 2000 and 2001 caused by the end of the dot-com bubble and a glut in production of silicon chips.

Manufacturing production in Scotland slumped by nearly 20 per cent in only two years. The economy has rarely experienced such a supply side shock. It is this meltdown in manufacturing which slowed growth rates and eroded productivity gains. Nevertheless, Scotland seemed to recover quickly, with only the odd quarter showing negative growth. This may be a statistical sleight of hand, as the Executive has radically altered the method of calculating quarterly economic growth to a series of moving averages, making longer-term comparisons more difficult. Thus recent higher quarterly growth figures are less an indication of economic vitality and more a reflection of a lower starting point, since the manufacturing base is being systematically downgraded in the construction of the growth index.

b) Employment

How has the labour market fared under devolution?

Evidence: The overall labour market has performed strongly over the devolution period, despite the loss of some 75,000 manufacturing jobs between 1999 and 2003. Unemployment and inactivity rates are historically low and for most of the period unemployment was below the UK average. International Labour Organisation (ILO) unemployment stood at 5.7 per cent at the beginning of 2005. Economic inactivity fell from 733,000 in 1999 to 662,000 in 2004, a drop of 20.6 per cent.

However, these rosy figures must be qualified. Rapid contraction in manufacturing jobs was offset only by a sharp rise in public sector jobs. The number of full-time employees in the state sector has risen from 408,041 to 444,500, with the biggest increase in local government, where councils employ 23,500 more people than when Labour came to power. By 2003, the number of people working in the public sector stood at 671,000 (using the Labour Force Survey figures), some 28 per cent of Scotland's 2,403,000 workforce.

There was also an absolute (and little heralded) rise in the inactivity levels of men aged 18–24 over the 1999–2004 period, suggesting the Executive's policies towards youth unemployment are not as effective as they claim. Above all, inactivity and unemployment rates vary enormously by region. The inactivity rate in Glasgow in 2003 exceeded 30 per cent.

Verdict: Scotland's relatively good employment performance (by historic standards) during the devolution period hides gross distortions in the labour market that the Executive has failed to address. Very likely the overall positive picture is a function of UK macroeconomic policies, a dynamic Edinburgh economy based on financial services growth, and the dramatic expansion of public sector jobs.

c) Exports

How has trade fared under devolution?

Evidence: Manufacturing export sales have fallen every single quarter (bar one) since the end of 2000 and are now nearly 40 per cent less in real terms then they were five years ago. In the core area of high technology, which normally constitutes the bulk of all Scottish manufacturing exports, sales have more than halved. Yet in 2004, world trade grew by the largest amount on record, 10.3 per cent in 12 months. The developing economies benefited most, but even the mature industrialized countries clocked up an average 8.3 per cent expansion in trade (including services). Scotland's manufacturing sector, with its emphasis on state-subsidized research, managed to decline through the biggest bull market in global trade we have seen. This suggests that something more is happening than a decline in traditional Scottish export markets.

Verdict: Manufacturing exports are seriously lower than pre-devolution.

d) Productivity

Scotland's poor economic growth record is a function of poor productivity by international standards. Productivity in Scotland is at least 35 per cent below the US in output per worker and 15–25 per cent less than Germany and France. According to data provided by Scottish Enterprise's skills unit in early 2005, output per employee is 8 per cent below the OECD average and 4 per cent below the UK average. Output per hour worked is 10 per cent below the OECD average and 5 per cent below the UK average. Has devolution improved this poor performance?

Evidence: The Office of National Statistics provides regional productivity data based on Gross Value Added (GVA) per hour worked. In 1996 and 1997, Scottish GVA per hour worked was 101.7 per cent of the UK. However, a fall in the index coincided with devolution: 99.4 in 1999, 98.6 in 2000, and 96.8 in 2001. This reflected the loss of highly productive manufacturing jobs and the introduction of less productive service jobs in the public sector. In 2002 there was a slight upturn to 97.2, and in 2003 to 98.1. The latter may reflect a worsening of UK productivity rather than any improvement in the Scottish situation.

Verdict: Productivity worse than pre-devolution.

2. Public expenditure and crowding out

The most glaring economic change brought about by devolution is the sharp increase in public expenditure and public sector employment.

Since 1999, public spending as a share of Scottish GDP has risen well above 50 per cent. In October 2005, Sir John Ward, the chairman of Scottish Enterprise, released the agency's own calculations suggesting the figure was now 55 per cent of gross value added (GDP less VAT and Customs duties). Calculating the share of state spending as a proportion of national income can be done in a number of ways and is an inexact science depending on the measures used and the relative allocation of non-area specific spending such as defence. However, all major commentators[1] are now agreed that the ratio of Scottish spending to GDP is over the 50 per cent mark. The average ratio of public spending to GDP for the OECD countries is in the low 40s. In Ireland the figure is around 33 per cent. London and the English south east, the most dynamic parts of the UK economy, are close to the Irish figure as are the USA and Australia.

Where has this money gone? Largely into wages and salaries. At the end of 2005 there were 36,500 more people employed full time by the Scottish Executive and local authorities than in 1997, a rise of 9 per cent. A figure that included quangos and public corporations would be closer to 11 per cent.

This situation carries with it the implicit danger the local economy will become unsustainable as a result of fiscal imbalances and real resource crowding out (where the low-productivity public sector starves the high-productivity private sector of labour and capital). A disproportionately large public sector bureaucracy can also lead to heavy regulation with its negative impact on private sector efficiency and business confidence.

Do any of these negatives apply to Scotland since devolution?

The case against crowding out in Scotland post-devolution is simple. State spending might account for up to 55 per cent

---

1   For a useful survey of the different calculations see David Smith, 'Does Britain Have Regional Justice, Or Injustice, in its Public Spending and Taxation?' Williams de Bros Economic Comment, October 2005.

of GDP but the level of taxation is far lower, probably at 43 per cent. The difference is filled by Treasury grants from London funded through the Barnett mechanism that ensures any spending rise in England is matched on a per capita basis in Scotland. This subvention is partly a subsidy by the rest of the UK and partly Treasury borrowing. However, in the case of Treasury borrowing, Scotland clearly enjoys the lower interest rates that UK economies of scale afford. In other words, this argument runs, the Executive is not imposing a fiscal burden on the local private sector as a result of the expansion of the state under devolution. Proof can be seen in the fact that the number of private jobs in Scotland is higher than pre-devolution, indicating little sign of crowding out.[2]

However this is not the end of the story. If classical crowding out does not seem to apply in Scotland (as of now) that does not mean to say that the vast growth in the state has been good for the economy. Making allowance for uncertainties in the official statistics, we can say that public spending equivalent to at least 10 per cent of Scottish GDP is being funded externally. No economy can escape the consequences of an inflow of expenditure equivalent to 10 per cent of GDP, particularly if the money is going largely into wages and salaries.

Typically, we would expect to see the following symptoms: a ballooning external trade deficit, a decline in exports, a poor record of domestic business start-ups, weakening international competitiveness and falling productivity, and asset price inflation particularly in urban property values. Do we see these symptoms in Scotland? As we saw in the first part of this chapter, all of these symptoms are seen in the Scottish economy and most have worsened since the devolution settlement.

---

2   However, unpublished ONS data suggests that in the year to October 2005 the overall number of private sector jobs in Scotland had started to decline – a hint that real resource crowding out has begun.

Evidence: Scotland runs a consistent trade deficit both with the UK and with the rest of the world combined. The precise data is hard to calculate but broad evidence is to hand in the Executive's own input–output tables for 2001. These show exports of £25.9 billion to rest of UK but imports amounting to £44.5 billion (including intermediate demand). And exports to the rest of the world of £24.2 billion but imports of £24.8 billion. In both cases there is a deficit but the internal one is clearly the biggest.

There are estimation problems with the input–output data and this choice of data is in contrast to the Executive's use of sampling to estimate exports and imports of goods and services. On this basis the Executive's April 2005 Scottish Economic Report claims that there was a trade surplus with the rest of the world in 2001. It lists exports at £23.4 billion which is in line with the £25.9 billion of the input–output approach. But it states imports at only £19.7 billion. This is at variance with the input–output approach by a fifth. It seems more probable that sampling data would understate the import bill.

Scottish foreign exports (less North Sea oil) were £19.5 billion in 2002, £18.8 billion in 2003, indicating a falling trend. Assuming foreign imports are still rising on the back of high consumer demand, this suggests a current foreign trade gap of between £6 and £9 billion.

The Executive has recently published some 'experimental' data on Scottish exports to the rest of the UK. These figures suggest Scottish exports of £33.3 billion for 2002 and £35.8 billion for 2003. That is a jump on the 2001 input–output tables. This might be explained by the success of Scottish financial intermediation services, which generated exports of £7.3 billion in 2002 and £7.5 billion in 2003. However, despite the growth of Scottish banking inside the UK, that still suggests a trade deficit between Scotland and the rest of the UK in the region of £11–12 billion.

Allowing for the crudeness of all these figures, Scotland is certainly running a hefty deficit that is only affordable because of the large public sector deficit. This has a direct knock-on effect on entrepreneurship. No major new Scottish company has emerged in the last decade (and most of those that emerged over the last 20–30 years have been the by-product of Thatcherite privatization and deregulation). Scotland's entrepreneurial dynamism, broadly captured by the number of start-ups per 100,000 people, consistently under-performs the UK average. Scotland relies heavily on spin-outs from the university and research sector rather than the company sector.

Verdict: If Scotland were a small Latin American economy the IMF would already have issued a dire warning about these dangerous economic symptoms. Where Scotland is different from our hypothetical South American economic disaster case is that the increase in state expenditure is not being financed by external borrowing. That has the advantage that the domestic interest rate is not rising and the exchange rate is not under pressure. However, just because the patient's temperature is not rising does not mean the virus is not eating away at the body.

What about Scandinavia?

The counter argument to this 'Latin American' thesis is to point out that many small European nations, particularly in Scandinavia, have high tax regimes with significant state sectors but, nevertheless, exhibit a higher growth and productivity record than Scotland. While this is superficially true, it cannot be accepted that economic performance is independent of the level of gross or marginal taxation, or the form of public spending, otherwise we are suggesting that cost and output bear no relationship to one another. In fact, on closer analysis, the Scottish and Scandinavian economies are radically different as a result of devolution. Therein lies the explanation for the differential impact of state finances on growth and productivity.

Unlike Scotland, the economies of the Scandinavian and Nordic nations, and of other successful small European countries such as Switzerland, are characterized by running large export surpluses. These are generated because of the existence of a premium manufacturing sector dominated in each country by major multinational companies; e.g. Nokia in Finland; Nestlé and Roche in Switzerland; Saab, Ericsson, Electrolux and ABB in Sweden. Between 2000 and 2003, Norway ran an average annual balance of payments surplus equivalent to 14 per cent of GDP, Switzerland 10 per cent, Finland 6.9 per cent and Sweden 4.6 per cent.

These large trade surpluses are ultimately what fund the large state sectors in these countries. They generate the company profits that pay the premium wages that support the high income taxes. Furthermore, as a general rule, domestic taxes on businesses and investment are low, encouraging a virtuous cycle of high investment. For instance, after the collapse of the Soviet Union, the Finns reacted to the loss of their traditional markets in Russia by abolishing taxes on personal dividend income and slashed profits tax on companies. That move attracted domestic savings into Finnish companies and paved the way for the rise of the mobile-phone giant, Nokia. Furthermore, the dominance of an advanced, multinational manufacturing sector ensures high productivity gains in these economies.

This analysis is not new and was first put forward by David Cameron[3] as long ago as 1978. Cameron's analysis of small, open economies in Europe demonstrated that openness to

---

3 David Cameron, 'The Expansion of the Public Economy: A Comparative Analysis', *American Political Science Review*, Vol. 72, No. 4 (1978), pp. 1,243–61; and David R. Cameron and Soo Yeon Kim, 'Trade, Political institutions, and the size of government', unpublished paper, Yale University, 2002.

international trade correlates highly with social spending levels that were exceptionally generous in small states. The reason was twofold. As noted above, generous balance of payment surpluses fund large state spending. But Cameron also argued that small open economies had to be extremely adaptable to global change and so put a premium on productivity gains. He further argued that a large state sector sometimes aided adaptability provided that expenditures promoted a social consensus that favoured change. Scotland does not fit the Cameron model. Not only is there no trade surplus but the large state expenditures that have followed devolution are used to fund conservative state institutions, and conservative public sector unions predominate in the system with a bias against manufacturing producers.

3. Policy critique

In this section we examine the rationale and consistency of the Executive's economic development strategy. This strategy consists of a turn towards domestic research and innovation and a de-prioritization of using foreign direct investment to construct branch assembly plants. It goes under the title *Smart, Successful Scotland*. A related aspect of this policy is a massive expansion in higher education to boost graduate numbers. We shall see that this policy direction does nothing to cope with the atypical Scottish model for a small European state – running a massive external deficit and a massive public sector.

Smart, Successful Scotland
Smart, Successful Scotland was launched in January 2001 by the then Enterprise Minister, Wendy Alexander, an MBA graduate from the prestigious INSEAD business school in

France. It had the strong backing of the First Minister, Henry McLeish, himself a development economist by profession and Alexander's predecessor as Enterprise Minister. Shorn of business jargon and multiple references to 'connectivity' and 'networks', the main thrust of the new policy was a switch from export manufacturing funded by inward investment and a new concentration on developing new, high-value products in our advanced universities, the latter filled with fee-paying foreign PhD students. Whatever its deficiencies, *Smart, Successful Scotland* represented the first proof that the Scottish Executive was taking economic policy seriously. It was not to last.

Alexander resigned from the Scottish Cabinet in May 2002, frustrated by the lack of support for her work from McLeish's replacement as First Minister, Jack McConnell, a former science teacher. McConnell replaced her with Iain Gray, a former community worker with no knowledge of business or the economy. (Gray would lose his Holyrood seat at the 2003 elections, after which McConnell relegated the Enterprise portfolio to his Liberal Democrat coalition partners, first in the shape of Jim Wallace and then Nichol Stephen.)

Smart, Successful Scotland was a curate's egg. It recognized correctly that globalization and the digital revolution had undermined reliance on FDI and branch plant manufacturing (much of which was already in meltdown following the collapse of the dot-com bubble). It paid lip service to the need for a domestic productivity revolution, though without saying how this was to be achieved. Above all, it created a buzz and had a galvanizing effect on business confidence.

Some flesh was put on the policy by the new head of the Scottish Enterprise development agency, Robert Crawford. He was professionally close to Alexander and championed the *Smart, Successful Scotland* strategy. Joining SE in early

2000, he reorganized its operations, sharply reducing the autonomy of the constituent local enterprise companies and re-focusing SE on a sectoral front rather than an area regeneration approach. These reforms created many internal enemies and led to Crawford's premature resignation in early 2004.

Crawford's flagship innovation was the creation of three Intermediate Technology Institutes (ITIs), for energy, biotechnology and information technology respectively. Using cash saved from SE's internal reorganization, a sum of £450 million over ten years would be allocated to the ITIs to invest in commercial research projects with a view to generating new products that could be licensed or manufactured in Scotland. This was a bold move though fraught with dangers. It smacked of picking winners. It would be 15 or 20 years before any major results were visible. It relied overmuch on university-oriented research. Above all, there was no obvious route by which the new products would be translated into Scottish jobs.

By the end of 2005, these problems were already manifesting themselves. The post-Crawford leadership at SE began interfering in the operations of the individual ITIs (which had been set up as stand-alone companies), prompting the resignation of two of the original three chief executives. SE's main board also began to hint at financial restrictions on ITI investments. However, the point is not whether the ITIs survive but that they are serving as a diversion from understanding that Scottish manufacturing – which drives national productivity growth and drives export sales – has been left to wither under devolution. The *de facto* policy of allowing low value-added manufacturing jobs to be off-shored to Asia while Scottish universities grow new high value-added knowledge industries for the future is too mechanical.

Evidence: According to CBI data, less than 20 per cent of UK manufacturing output is generated by new product launches – in Germany, the figure is more like half. In other words, *Smart, Successful Scotland* is misguided because we are poor at turning new ideas into sellable products, due in part to our anti-manufacturing, public-sector bias. That bias is being reinforced by the massive expansion of the Scottish public sector. The issue is not the lack of ideas and patents but the lack of large-enough firms and qualified management to engage in manufacturing export competition with Scandinavia and (soon) China.

Verdict: Five years on, *Smart, Successful Scotland* has produced no important improvement in Scottish productivity, no new manufacturing firms of more than 250 workers, and no major commercializations of Scottish research.

Higher education

One area where *Smart, Successful Scotland* has had a measurable impact is in the university sector, where Scotland has a comparative advantage over many other small industrial nations. Between 1999 and 2003, there was a 30 per cent increase in the funding of Scottish Higher Education. Scotland also has the highest graduation rate as a percentage of the population of all the OECD countries: some 51.5 per cent of young people enter higher and further education before they are 21.

How does this square with the failure to raise Scottish productivity or manufacturing exports? The explanation for this paradox can be found in a new piece of research[4] by two American economists, Philippe Aghion of Harvard and Peter Howitt of Brown University. They have re-examined the

---

4   Philippe Aghion and Peter Howitt, 'Appropriate Growth Policy: A Unifying Framework'. Harvard University website, www.harvard.edu.

productivity revolution in the United States during the 1990s, trying to understand why new technology raised US economic performance while European (and Scottish) productivity stagnated by comparison.

The answer, according to Aghion and Howitt, has to do with how an economy combines education and technology. The closer an economy is to the technological frontier, the more growth is dependent on a university-educated workforce. This is not because the technology is complex but because getting the most out of the information technology revolution requires a cultured, flexible workforce. On the other hand, economies further back on the technology frontier – those with a greater emphasis on process industries – need more emphasis on good secondary education to create a disciplined, numerate, technically skilled workforce.

According to Aghion and Howitt, America won the IT war because of its huge competitive advantage in graduates. Europe, on the other hand, was ahead during the period 1950–80, because of its superior secondary education that fitted the technology (and associated business culture) of that earlier period. Some 31 per cent of Americans have a degree, the highest proportion in the world, while only a quarter of Europeans do. For the UK, the figure is 20 per cent (according to the latest OECD figures, for 2001). But despite *Smart, Successful Scotland*, only 16 per cent of the Scottish workforce has a degree, putting the country in 17th place among the industrial countries. Even Ireland has a bigger percentage of graduates than Scotland.

How can Scotland have so few graduates in the workforce despite sending over 50 per cent of young people into some form of higher or further education? The answer is that the many graduates emigrate. In other words, while the Scottish Executive has been obsessed with graduate numbers (i.e. process) it failed to notice that the actual graduate population in the workforce was Third World standard (i.e. outcome) – which goes to the heart of Scotland's poor productivity record.

Evidence: A study[5] by the London Economics consultancy, in April 2003, found that investment in information and communications technologies (ITC) in Scotland was adding close to 0.6 percentage points to annual productivity growth for the years 1992–2001. However, this compared unfavourably to the UK figure of 0.76 percentage points per annum (which accounted for 47 per cent of the total annual UK average increase in labour productivity). Here is a smoking gun that indicates that Scotland, despite its significant higher education system, is in fact failing to generate productivity gains from new technology. The London Economics report also showed that other UK regions outperformed Scotland. Predictably, the average ICT contribution to labour productivity growth in London was 1.16 percentage points per annum, but even the English north west outdid Scotland with an ICT contribution to productivity of 0.7 percentage points per annum.

The comparative failure at graduate level is mirrored at the secondary level. One in eight Scots between the ages of 16 and 24 has no qualifications whatsoever, and 18 per cent of today's young Scots have never had a job or gone on to higher education. This situation remains despite the increase in public spending on education under devolution. The reason for this failure is twofold. First, the misplaced emphasis on getting yet more young people into university. Second, the failure of the Executive to abandon the failed comprehensive school (as they have done in England) in favour of German-style vocational streaming.

5　'ITC Investment and Productivity in the UK: a Regional Assessment', *London Economics*, April 2002.

Verdict: Under devolution, we have sacrificed technical education for the non-academic majority on the altar of getting half our young folk into university. But we've gained little to date because our graduates emigrate to grow the London economy. Scotland has neither the correct workforce for German-style manufacturing nor for high-tech US service industries.

4. Conclusions

The first six years of devolution have been a wasted opportunity as far as economic policy is concerned. Despite protestations that economic growth was going to be top of the agenda, the administration of Jack McConnell has failed to deliver in any sustainable fashion. *Smart, Successful Scotland* was more of a signpost than a detailed policy subscription. Increased spending on the universities, while welcome, has still to improve Scotland's lamentably poor graduate skills base. Nothing fundamental has been done to improve productivity. Above all, the collapse in manufacturing exports has been ignored.

The key thing to grasp is that off-shoring manufacturing as a strategy is wrong. We need to manufacture here, and manufacture as much as possible. Scotland needs to follow the path of cities such as Aberdeen, which used the proximity of the North Sea oil industry to create a new generation of Scottish engineering companies. Less than 1.5 per cent of the gross value added by Scotland's current top 100 companies comes from businesses in technology-based sectors such as IT hardware, chemicals, pharmaceutical and biotechnology, aerospace and defence, electrical and electronic engineering, telecommunications services, software and computer services. This is where we need to concentrate.

Small engineering companies and start-ups are not enough. Scotland needs to create its own global engineering players. That is obviously easier said than done. But we might start by promoting engineering education at secondary and graduate level; by focusing on our offshore oil engineering industry as a jumping off point; by reviving our defunct inward investment strategies, especially in regard to pharmaceuticals and chemicals; by ordering a new generation of nuclear power stations built in Scotland; and by funding technology demonstrators such as a state-of-the-art bullet train between Glasgow and Edinburgh. Ultimately the entrepreneurial spark will have to come from the private sector, but the Executive can redefine itself as an enabler whose primary job is to build a consensus for economic development.

Unlike European regional governments, the political leadership of the Executive has been backward looking and focused on redistribution and social justice issues rather than looming economic problems. This is all too understandable given the vast subsidies that flowed from London as Chancellor Gordon Brown raised taxes. But the result has further exacerbated the Scottish trade deficit and placed the sustainability of the economy on a perilous footing. One thing is for sure: if the devolved Parliament and Executive do not raise economic issues to a higher priority, then the current constitutional half-way-house will not survive. Which path Scotland then follows is for history to decide.

*   *   *

George Kerevan, associate editor of *The Scotsman* since 2000, previously held numerous academic posts with Napier University. He is a former member of Edinburgh City Council, and has served on many arts and civic boards. He is a former member of the SNP National Council and SNP environment spokesman. Freelance activities include broadcasting, film making and public speaking.

DONALD MACKAY

4

How global forces will compel economic change

Introduction

The chattering classes are fond of expressing concern as to the 'competitive threat' of the global economy. Competition there will certainly be. But anyone brought up in the tradition of Adam Smith (this, unfortunately, excluding most Scots) will understand that competition is one of the great motors of economic development. The growth of the global economy will open up all the advanced economies to more competition and the developing economies will grow more rapidly than the advanced economies. This has been the way of the 'modern' world for more than three centuries. But, while the chattering classes often perceive international trade as a zero sum game, the evidence of history demonstrates it is a two-way street – or, at least, it is for those with the wit and energy to respond to the opportunities it presents.

This general comment applies to Scotland, a regional economy within the UK economy, as it does to any other advanced economy. The economic history of Scotland in the period since the Union of the Parliaments is one of seeking to participate on a wider playing field. When this has been successful and the playing field has widened, Scots have benefited from the process. In periods when trade barriers have become more important, the Scottish economy has struggled – most notably in the period from 1914 to the end of the Second World War. Again, this is part of a wider pattern – small economies benefit particularly from freer trade and suffer particularly from greater protectionism.

Today, we stand at the threshold of an era, which, for the first time in history, is witnessing the growth of a truly global economy. That is, a largely market-driven economy which now embraces the two most populous countries of the world, China and India, and, alongside them, a range of large and small economies in the Far East and Eastern Europe. Given the scale of these countries and their potential for rapid and sustained development, the next few decades are likely to see very rapid growth on a global basis.

From local to national and international

Three centuries ago Scotland was a small, essentially agrarian economy, poor by the standards of north-west Europe. Her businesses, hampered by geography, lacked good access to the richer markets of England and her emerging colonial markets. Scotland's trade with north-west Europe was culturally and socially important, but limited in scope.

The Darien Disaster was a brave but doomed attempt to escape from this economic straitjacket and a major factor in increasing support for the Union of 1707. Over the ensuing three decades the economic results of the Union were disappointing, to say the least, as Scottish businesses struggled to compete with their more efficient English counterparts. There followed the troika of miracles – the Enlightenment, the Agricultural Revolution and the Industrial Revolution. As a consequence of these, Scotland became a fully paid-up member of the industrialized British economy and the emerging international economy.

Specialization of labour and money transfers within a wider geography replaced much of the self-sufficiency and barter that had characterized economic activity at a local level. To be effective, the specialization of labour required a revolution in transport systems. This established an integrated domestic economy, while the rapidly developing trans-Atlantic trade created the cotton and tobacco merchants of Glasgow. In the nineteenth century the flows of trans-Atlantic trade and capital help to explain much of the growth and the trade cycle evident in the domestic economy. By the 1870s Britain was the 'workshop of the world' and Glasgow was 'the second city of the Empire'. Although the UK's industrial pre-eminence came under severe challenge from Continental Europe from 1870, and from the US subsequently, Scotland remained an important international centre dependent on the 'heavy industries' of shipbuilding, engineering, steel and coal.

The progression, from local to national and international, transformed the standard of living that could be enjoyed in the industrialized world. Thus, the economist, John Maynard Keynes, could write of the period just before the First World War:

> The inhabitant of London (he could as well have written Glasgow or Edinburgh) could order by telephone, sipping his morning tea in bed, the various products of the whole earth . . . and reasonably expect their early delivery upon his doorstep; . . . he could at the same moment and by the same means adventure his wealth in the natural resources and new enterprises of any quarter of the world, and share, without exertion or even trouble, in their prospective fruits and advantages. (*The Economic Consequences of the Peace*, 1919)

The behaviour Keynes was describing was largely confined to higher-income groups, mostly in the industrialized economies of the West. Yet, there was, in everyday behaviour and in the ebb and flow of business life, an unmistakable international current. An economy, defined almost exclusively in terms of local activity, had long since given way to one in which national and international markets were increasingly important.

As Keynes had feared, among 'the economic consequences of the peace' after the First World War were recession, protectionism and heavy unemployment. World trade was severely inhibited and economic growth became heavily dependent on the 'new industries' responding to domestic rather than international demand. This was not an economic climate helpful to a Scottish economy much more dependent on external demand, and Scotland experienced high and prolonged unemployment through most of the inter-war period.

International, world and global economies

The world trade which characterized the international economy of the pre-1914 era was largely restricted to foodstuffs, raw materials and a narrow range of manufactured products. But the peace settlement post-1945, strongly influenced by Keynes and pushed through by American muscle, was explicitly designed to build a new and wider international economic order. The key institutional change was the creation of the General Agreement on Tariffs and Trade (GATT) which sought to reduce tariff barriers, based on the principles of reciprocity, non-discrimination and transparency.

GATT was highly effective in reducing the tariff barriers of the major industrial economies, as demonstrated by the decline in average tariff barriers on manufactured goods negotiated through the GATT 'rounds'.

Figure 1: GATT rounds; decline in industrial country tariffs

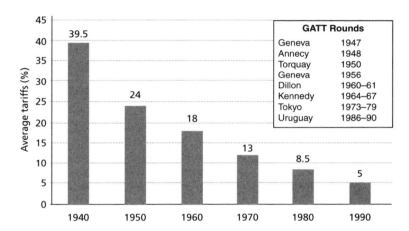

As a consequence of reduced tariff barriers, world trade increased more rapidly than world income over the quarter of a century from 1950, as the major economies became more open (see Figure 2). However, the difference between these growth rates narrowed over time. In fact, GATT (now replaced by the World Trade Organization) was much more effective in reducing manufacturing tariffs than in liberalizing trade in agriculture and in services, the latter being an increasingly important element in world trade. The World Trade Organization continues to have the same difficulty.

Even within manufacturing, world trade in textiles, clothing, steel, cars, shoes, machinery and consumer electronics was restricted by Voluntary Export Restraints (VERs), the term 'voluntary' being used in the time-honoured military sense. Indeed, the growth in foreign direct investment, which was so marked in the 1980s and which continued into the

Figure 2: Change in world trade and output (%)

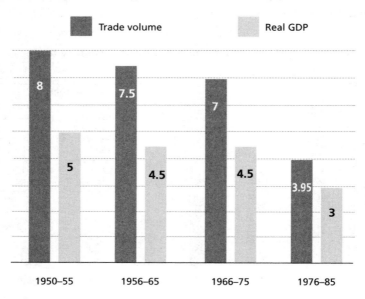

1990s, was due, in part, to a need to get behind tariff and non-tariff barriers in a range of manufacturing and service industries. Nonetheless, the reduced barriers to trade in manufacturing goods was sufficient to allow the very rapid expansion of the Asian Tiger economies from 1970 – these including Hong Kong, Malaysia, South Korea, Singapore and Taiwan. Over 1970–90 the growth rate of industrial production for South Korea was some five times that for the advanced industrial countries as a whole.

In the 1990s the growth of world trade continued to be higher than the growth of world income, but a large element of this faster growth was within customs unions, particularly within the European Union. Another major change in the 1990s was the collapse of international communism as a credible ideology. Frank Fukujama labelled this the 'end of history', meaning that, as a system of governance, liberal democracy, based on individual property rights and the rule of law, should be viewed as the end of an evolutionary process, rather than a staging post on the route to some other form of political organization. Within the evident overstatement there is a serious point. Many of the countries liberated from communist ideology actively seek political ties and trading relationships with the liberal democracies and look to them for their model of government. As a consequence, there has been a large increase in the number of countries seeking to join a world order based on mainly market-led economies and freer trade.

The shape of the future

The shape of the global economy will be heavily influenced, even dominated, by China and India. China's economy has being growing for some two decades at an average annual rate of some 8 per cent. Suppose this were to continue through to 2050, and suppose that the other economies in the following illustration continued their recent growth rates, then their respective GDPs in 2050 would be as shown in Figure 3.

A G8 constructed on this basis would have three new members – China, India and Brazil – and would lose Canada, France and Italy. Moreover, the top three economies, containing the new giants of China and India, along with the USA, would dominate the global economy.

The first question is: does this picture depict a plausible scenario? Well, it is based on extrapolating past trends over a very long period and my statistics lecturer was fond of exclaiming that 'extrapolation is a substitute for thinking'. Yet, these developing economies do share features which have resulted in the sustained and rapid growth of developing

Figure 3: Ten largest economies in 2050

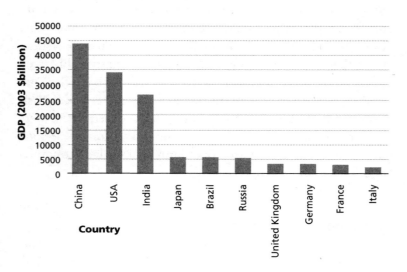

economies in the past. That is, they have large reservoirs of labour in very low productivity activities (mainly subsistence agriculture) which will migrate readily to urban areas and whose productivity can be transformed by appropriate education and training programmes and the application of known technology. Political problems may derail economic growth temporarily, but it is difficult to refute the notion that these are Asian giants who, within this century, and probably over the next few decades, will transform themselves and, thereby, the global economy.

There are two broad responses to this issue. One is that depicted by the courtiers of King Canute who believed that their king could hold back the elemental forces of nature. The other is depicted by the king who knew he did not have the power to do so. Scotland is in the latter position. In the jargon of the economist, she is a 'price taker rather than a price fixer', i.e. the Scottish economy has to respond to an external economic environment over which she has no appreciable influence.

Look at Figure 3 again and remember that Scotland accounts for less than 10 per cent of UK GDP. She is a small fish in a large pool, and that pool is about to get much larger. Whatever policy is adopted, the Scottish economy will get relatively smaller. Yet, because the economic opportunities unleashed by the global economy will be so huge, they will create large economic gains for those economies which can respond to them. So, are we well equipped for the task?

Stands Scotland where she did?

Globalization is a further stage in the international special-ization of labour. Such specialization requires more, not less international trade. To share fully in the benefits from this process, any region needs a range of activities which are capable of competing effectively in external markets.

This has been Scotland's critical weakness. She has a set of financial services businesses which are internationally com-petitive by any standards. But she is weak in other tradeable services and the manufacturing base (which is export inten-sive) is shrinking. This is particularly evident in recent years, above all in the electronics industry, which was one of the inward investment success stories. The Scottish business base is very small and her competitive position has continued to weaken since devolution, both domestically and in wider international markets.

Let us look at the Scottish economy within the UK context first, and then consider the wider implications. Measured by GDP per capita, Scotland is in the middle range of OECD countries. Within the UK, Scotland is the fourth wealthiest of 13 UK regions. As the OECD embraces the richest economies of the world, and as the UK is one of those economies, it would be foolish to make extravagant claims that the present position is wholly unsatisfactory. Yet past performance hardly warrants complacency, which is the one commodity in excess supply in the current policy making.

The best single indicator of an economy's overall economic growth is the increase in total GDP. Figure 4 shows the percentage annual increase for Scotland and the rest of the UK (RUK) over 1970–2004.

Figure 4: Annual percentage change in real GDP, 1970–2004

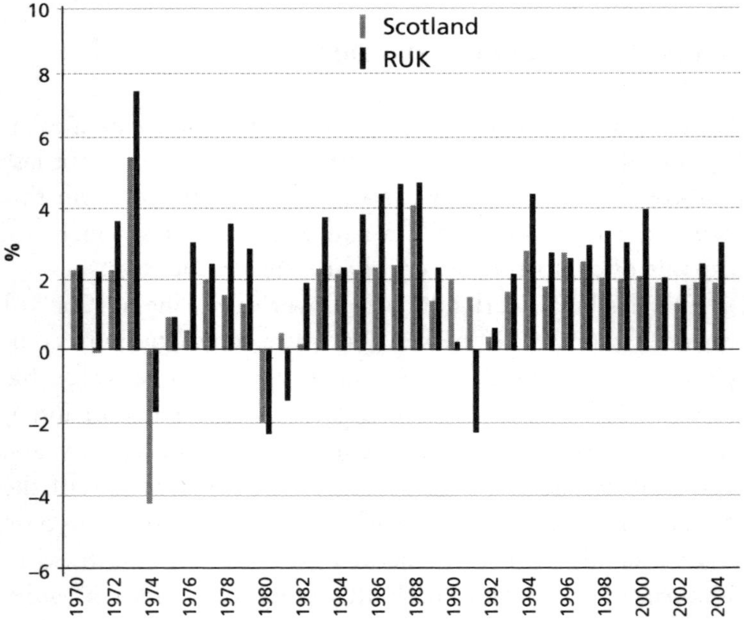

In the 35-year period the percentage annual growth (or, rarely, decline) of total Scottish GDP compares favourably with that for RUK in only six of 35 years – these being 1975, 1980–81, 1991–92 and 1996. For most five-year periods the average increase in Scottish GDP is only some 70 per cent of

RUK GDP. This is not to say that living standards have fallen relatively. On the contrary, Scottish GDP per capita, as a percentage of UK GDP per capita, has been remarkably steady over this period. Put simply, Scotland has generated less additional economic activity than the rest of the UK, but relative living standards have changed very little as substantial numbers of Scots left to find better opportunities elsewhere. To put this another way, Scotland 'exported' her unemployment problem.

The sharpest contrast within the UK economy is between London and the south east on the one hand, and the rest of the UK economy on the other. It is sometimes alleged that the prosperity of the former is due to the fact that it is the seat of UK government. But the real strength of the south east is that it has a much stronger business base and a much more entrepreneurial climate than the rest of the UK. Moreover, the UK has long enjoyed a form of functional finance which uses the economic strength of the south east to redistribute income on a regional as well as on a personal basis. A progressive tax structure, plus the notion that public services should be of a similar quality across all regions, redistributes income from London and the south east to all the other UK regions. And Scotland has been a major beneficiary of this process.

Let us look at the standing of the Scottish economy in the regional context before devolution, then move on to considering what has changed since. If one takes 1997–98 as a typical year (it was) then one finds that for eight regions (Wales and the English regions, except London and the rest of the south east) there was a clear tendency for identifiable public expenditure per capita to rise as regional per capita income fell. However, the differences in public expenditure per capita were not particularly large for these regions – so the system was mildly redistributive in favour of the poorer regions. Amongst these regions, those with similar per capita incomes received roughly similar public expenditure settlements.

The 'outlying' regions were the south east (excluding London), London, Northern Ireland and Scotland. For the south east (excluding London) public expenditure per capita was higher than one might 'expect' given its higher per capita income, but still lower than that in most other regions. By way of contrast, London, Northern Ireland and Scotland all enjoyed much higher public expenditure per capita than any other region. In London's case this reflects 'congestion' costs and it should be borne in mind that this region has a very large surplus of taxation revenue over public expenditure.

Turning to Scotland, the figures in the table illustrate the favourable treatment she enjoyed relative to Wales (a region with lower per capita income) and the East Midlands (a region with very similar per capita income). GDP is expressed as a percentage of the UK level.

GDP (% of UK) and identifiable public expenditure per capita, 1997–98

	GDP (%)	Expenditure (£)
Scotland	95.5	6,006
Wales	82.2	5,625
East Midlands	95.9	4,770

Source: Ross MacKay, 'The Search for Balance: Taxing and Spending Across the United Kingdom', Institute of Welsh Affairs, 2001.

On the latest available data (for 2003) the relationships depicted here have not changed appreciably in recent years and, by 1997–98, the relationships were already longstanding, at least so far as they applied to Scotland. The 'Barnett Formula', devised during the earlier devolutionary debate of the 1970s, was intended to reduce through time the comparative advantage that Scotland then enjoyed in terms of public expenditure. In practice, various devices were employed to subvert its apparent inexorable arithmetic. Hence, over a period of 20 years prior to devolution, Scotland enjoyed a relatively high level of expenditure and, post-devolution, that relative position has not changed appreciably. What has changed is that post-2000 public expenditure as a percentage of national income has risen more rapidly for the UK than for any other OECD country and Scotland has shared fully in this process. As a percentage of GDP, public expenditure in Scotland is now above 50 per cent, some 10 per cent above the UK equivalent.

The effect on the Scottish economy is akin to the sensation experienced by a frog as the water temperature rises. It is quite pleasant at first, but a feeling of initial well-being can result in very unpleasant longer-term consequences. Very rapid increases in public expenditure, starting from a high base, have resulted in large increases in public sector employment in Scotland, much smaller increases in private sector employment and lower unemployment. This is unsurprising. As Keynes remarked some 70 years ago, if there is a margin of unused capacity in the economy then increased public expenditure can have a favourable impact on employment, even when the initial expenditure is itself unproductive:

If the Treasury were to fill old bottles with banknotes, bury them at suitable depths in disused coalmines . . . and leave it to private enterprise . . . to dig the notes up again there need be no more unemployment. (*The General Theory of Employment, Interest and Money*, 1936)

This is not to suggest that an increase in public expenditure is necessarily unproductive as in this example. Healthcare and general education, the two categories of public expenditure

which have risen fastest, are public goods and it is appropriate
that they should be mainly publicly funded. Yet, the evidence is
that much of this increased expenditure has raised the cost base
of the public sector with no commensurate increase in outputs.
At a UK level, the rate of price inflation in the public sector has
been much higher than price inflation in the private sector over
a number of years. As salaries are the main element of cost in
public services, this must mean that salaries have been increasing more rapidly and/or that productivity increases lag behind
those in the private sector. There is no reason to believe that
Scotland is immune to this process and quite a few reasons to
suggest that this process is more marked for Scottish public
services.

The actions, as distinct from the 'spin' of the Scottish
Executive, show no sign that the efficiency and growth of the
economy are an important objective of higher public spending. As one authority has concluded from a review of Scottish
Executive expenditure and policy actions, 'The most plausible conclusion is that the priority to economic development
is not an effective priority' (Peter Wood, Fraser of Allander
Institute, June 2005).

It is a matter of arithmetic that the rapid increase in public
expenditure in Scotland must have been accompanied by a
substantial deterioration in Scotland's trade balance with the
rest of the world (this including RUK). A recent study has
suggested that Scotland is the only region in the UK to have
experienced a substantial deterioration in her competitiveness
over 1997–2005, her competitive ranking falling from fourth
to eighth of 12 regions over this period (Robert Huggins
Associates, UK Competitiveness Index, 2005). The main
factor behind this has been the decline in manufacturing
employment and, above all, the sharp reduction in electronics
output and exports. But Scotland also scores badly across the
other main indicators of business competitiveness.

The outstanding weakness is that the business base is small relative to the size of the economy. The best measure of this, VAT registered businesses per 10,000 inhabitants, has been some 15 per cent below the British average since these data first became available (see *Scotland's Enterprise Deficit*, published by the Policy Institute, 2001). This discrepancy is concentrated in the central belt of Scotland and business density is much lower than in other comparable UK regions.

There has been no improvement post-devolution. On the contrary, the competitive deficit has widened appreciably (see Huggins *op. cit.* Table 2.19). This is confirmed by a recent study for the CBI conducted by Grant Thornton, which shows that, over 1994–2004, the stock of VAT registered businesses rose by only half the UK rate (5 per cent plays 10 per cent). The Scottish growth rate is lower still in the period since devolution.

None of this can be any great surprise. The Scottish Executive appears to believe that its main *raison d'être* is to promote the public interest by administering a much higher level of public spending, with little regard to the efficiency of that spend or the welfare of the business base. It is difficult to demonstrate, in any particular case, that public expenditure has 'crowded out' private-sector activity. But it is even more difficult to resist this conclusion in Scotland's case. An American study of the developed industrial nations found that reducing the public employment sector wage bill as a percentage of GDP has a strong positive impact on private investment (see Alesina *et al.*, *The American Economic Journal*, 2002). And Scotland is at the extreme end of the range in terms of the public sector's share of the total wage bill!

Although the evidence is from underdeveloped economies, it might also be worth pondering the following quotation which has a clear resonance in our experience since devolution:

The accumulation in little more than a decade of even a small proportion of the workforce in an unproductive 'sink' can sap the economy of its dynamism, eliminating improvements in living standards for all but the few who obtain rent-yielding jobs. (Gelb *et al.*, *Economic Journal*, 1991)

The 'sink' referred to is the public sector and the proposition is that if that sector increases with little accompanying productivity gain, then those who gain from this process are mainly employed in the public sector. On the available evidence since devolution, it would be difficult to argue the proposition that Scotland is a rare exception to this general rule.

Conclusions

The development of China and India will profoundly change the scale and nature of the global economy and will require major changes in the structure of the developed, as well as in the structure of the developing economies. The former will experience much greater effective competition across a wide range of activities, particularly those which are labour intensive and with relatively fixed technology. Yet there are parallel opportunities to these threats.

A country which only exported would rapidly build up its foreign exchange reserves, but would simultaneously depress the living standards of its own people. Sooner or later, and it is usually sooner rather than later, the major part of export earnings will be reflected in growing imports of goods and services and/or in the export of capital invested in other economies. The major part of this new flow of demand will accrue to the developed world. Hence the statement, at the beginning of this paper, that international trade is a two-way street. However, the developed economies who will benefit from this process will require a range of business sector activities capable of competing effectively in the global economy. With some honourable exceptions, the Scottish business base presently lacks the width and variety of businesses which can compete effectively in this environment.

Scotland will be a smaller fish in a much larger pool. That is not in doubt whatever policies Scotland adopts. Nor can any of this be laid at the door of devolution. All the main trends sketched in above would have happened in the absence of devolution. Yet, the manner in which devolution is currently operating is certainly not helpful to the major restructuring that the economy requires.

The cost of government has increased substantially – more politicians living at the taxpayers' expense, more ministers and more ministerial offices, a badly mismanaged and extremely expensive parliament building and a substantial increase in the accompanying bureaucracy. Moreover, as far as economic policy is concerned, there is no corresponding benefit in terms of an improved policy framework. As one knowledgeable insider put it, 'In the past our policy papers were poorly presented, almost scruffy in appearance, but any sensible person could understand what we are saying and what we were trying to do. Today they are glossy, very long and free of any coherent thought or policy initiative'.

The American economist, J. K. Galbraith, famously drew a distinction between private affluence and public squalor in the US economy of the 1950s. Scotland is in a very different situation. The public sector is very large, affluent and comparatively inefficient. The private sector, which is the source of the goods and services which might be required by the rapidly developing economies of the world, is comparatively efficient but, relatively, very small. To borrow a phrase used to describe the UK economy in the 1970s, Scotland has 'too few producers'. Scotland is much further down this road than the UK was in the 1970s.

This is not a good starting position to compete efficiently in the global economy. Yet, ironically, the reduction in tariff barriers and the emergence of the global economy would appear to be particularly beneficial to smaller economies (Alisina and Spolaore, *The Size of Nations*). Although this study is set in the context of nation states, the underlying argument is equally applicable at a regional level.

If there is a serious wish to build a more competitive Scottish economy, then the first requirement is to halt the rapid growth of public expenditure. At present there is much talk of 'cuts' in public expenditure at a UK, as well as a Scottish level. In reality, this usually means that public expenditure is expected to grow more slowly than in the past and still faster than in the economy as a whole. What Scotland needs, over a significant period of time, is a much stricter rule – let us call it a 'golden rule' – that public expenditure should grow below the growth rate of national income over a period of years.

To accomplish this, the Scottish Executive has to find a means of encouraging the birth and development of new businesses. The problem is too widespread, and most of the businesses too small, for this to be best accomplished through direct intervention by government agencies. On the evidence, the most effective means is to reduce business taxes. A review of the international evidence over almost three decades suggests that a reduction of corporate taxes of 10 per cent increases the annual growth rate of an economy by 2 per cent (*Journal of Public Economics*, June 2005).

Possibly of even greater relevance to Scotland is the specific experience of Ireland. Both the domestic and the international observers of the 'Irish Miracle' are convinced that the critical enabling factor was the highly favourable corporation tax regime. A regime which, incidentally was, and still is, accompanied by relatively high personal taxation.

Cutting corporation tax is not within the gift of the Scottish Parliament, but there are two means of lowering taxes which should be considered. The first, using the discretionary power of the Scottish Parliament to lower the standard rate of income tax, is likely to be the more politically popular, but may not be particularly effective. The costs of tax collection would be relatively high and the tax reduction would not be specifically directed toward correcting the imbalance between the public and private sectors of the economy. Moreover, it would likely be wildly unpopular with English taxpayers who already contribute generously toward funding the high level of public expenditure in Scotland.

The second possibility would be to reduce local business taxation. Thus far, the contribution of the Scottish Executive in this area has been muddled and extremely unhelpful. Having lobbied over many years to obtain uniform rates across the economy, before devolution, Scottish business then saw this, first, thrown away. The Executive then declared it would return to a situation of equality – although the timing of this remains uncertain. This 'Grand Old Duke of York' approach is hopelessly inadequate. The small business base in Scotland is longstanding and shows no signs of yielding to the traditional 'cures'. The evidence is telling us that if we are to address the issue seriously we need to have a measure in place which will reduce business costs significantly. There also needs to be a reasonable assurance that this system will remain in place over a substantial period of time.

For example, it would be sensible to announce that the Scottish Executive would plan to reduce the business rate by, say, 25 per cent a year over a four-year period and intend, thereafter, to maintain a zero rate for a further six-year period. This would give the Executive time to execute the efficiency savings it claims to have identified without any reduction in the quality of public services. More realistically, it would be a wake-up call to undertake a real search for efficiency gains!

Such a policy measure is well suited to attacking the most important features of the underlying problem. It would certainly reduce the start-up costs of new businesses and the running costs of such businesses once established, as property costs are known to be particularly important in both circumstances. This being so, it could be expected to increase the birth rate and the survival rate of new businesses, these being the critical weaknesses established by the evidence. This would require a sharp reduction in the rate of growth of the Scottish Budget and enforce greater efficiency in the use of public money, but both are essential if we are to restructure our economy.

It might be argued that it does not make sense to respond to a global challenge by reducing local taxation, but the policy would give real meaning to the phrase, 'think local, act global'. Further it could be contended that it would take years for such a policy to be effective. I would have to plead guilty as charged. After all, it has taken us years to create an economy so heavily dependent on a relatively inefficient public sector and not well suited to benefit from the developing global economy. The Executive can do relatively little to assist those larger companies who are already active in global markets, but the proposed policy is certainly not inimical to some of the important location decisions of those companies and is directly relevant to refreshing and expanding the existing business base.

We should be clear. We can continue with present policies and probably be reasonably comfortable in terms of our living standards, so long as the present high level of public expenditure can be sustained. However, we cannot reasonably expect this benign situation to continue for very long and it will not help us to build an economy more suited for the competitive pressures and opportunities of the global market. In a European Union, within which so many of the member states pursue low growth so diligently, Scotland would not be an exception. However, if we want to participate fully in the global economy, we must create a culture which will rectify the present imbalance between the private and the public sectors. This requires a very different attitude of mind and a very different policy emphasis to those presently on display.

*   *   *

Professor Sir Donald MacKay is one of Scotland's most eminent economists. He was Professor of Economics at Heriot-Watt University and Professor of Political Economy at Aberdeen University. He is a former chairman of Scottish Enterprise (1993–97) and of the Malcolm Group. He is Governor of the National Institute of Economic and Social Research, chairman of Scottish Mortgage Investment Trust and Director of Edinburgh Income and Value Trust.

Politics and the Constitution

GERALD WARNER

5

Devolved Scotland: Britain's Potemkin village

'THE SCOTTISH PARLIAMENT, which adjourned on the 25th day of March in the year 1707, is hereby reconvened.' With those words Winifred Ewing, as 'mother' of the devolved Scottish Parliament, opened its first sitting after the swearing-in of MSPs, on 12 May 1999. It was a complete misrepresentation of reality.

The historic Scottish Parliament was not adjourned in 1707: it was superseded by the Parliament of Great Britain. Prior to that it was the national parliament of Scotland, sovereign under the Crown. The parliament over which Mrs Ewing was presiding is a devolved assembly with certain powers delegated by Westminster, which has the authority to constrain, expand or rescind them at any time. The Scottish Parliament does not have jurisdiction over social security, defence, foreign policy, macroeconomics or other matters reserved to Westminster by the Scotland Act. It is in no sense the pre-Union Parliament reconvened.

Mrs Ewing confided to her euphoric audience that she had always wanted to make that announcement. Therein lay the explanation, not only of her personal fantasy, but of the many other absurdities associated with the Scottish Parliament project. It is a forum of wishful thinking, grudge romanticism and self-indulgence. If MSPs wish something were the case, they persuade themselves that it is so and act accordingly. Illusion is devolution's life-support system. Devolved Scotland is a Potemkin village. This mentality derives from the history of the whole devolution project, which was not, as pretended, a product of the national will but was always pure hype, artificially engineered by a small group of politicians and media folk.

History of the devolution project

Although there had often been small groups of romantics agitating for some form of Scottish devolution, these had always been fringe elements. An early example was the 'Justice to Scotland' movement, officially called the National Association for the Vindication of Scottish Rights, created in 1853 by the High Tory Earl of Eglinton (of tournament fame). This had the modest objectives of restoring the post of Secretary of State for Scotland and the other boards and offices that had been abolished – although guaranteed by the Treaty of Union – larger financial grants to Scotland, an increase in Parliamentary seats and better maintenance of the neglected royal palaces and parks. Infiltration by separatists provoked its dissolution. In the twentieth century, such romantics usually gravitated to the Scottish National Party, although the exploitation of North Sea oil in the 1970s turned that into a mass movement of unambiguously socialist character.

It was in the 1960s, and specifically in response to the SNP's by-election victory at Hamilton in 1967, that politicians within the two major parties were panicked into devising some form of appeasement, short of separatism, that might seduce moderate voters away from nationalism. The Conservative Party blinked first. The Thistle Group of Scottish Tories and the internal committee set up under Sir William McEwan Younger to study Scottish government were straws in the wind. It was Edward Heath who sold the pass with his so-called 'Declaration of Perth' in 1968 – delivered without consultation with his Scottish party – creating the public mood that would eventually devour Scottish Toryism. A Scottish Constitutional Committee chaired by Sir Alec Douglas Home reported in 1970 in favour of a directly elected Scottish 'Convention' with 125 members, sitting in Edinburgh to process the intermediate stages of Scottish legislation. The party conference approved this in May 1970.

Labour by then had given in to the prevailing political mood and Harold Wilson set up a Royal Commission on the Constitution. The Tory government of 1970–74 did not effect constitutional change, partly because of its preoccupation with local government reform and partly due to its problems with industrial relations. In 1973 the party conference threw out the devolution proposals it had previously supported, but later that year the Royal Commission inherited from Wilson produced the Kilbrandon Report, offering various devolutionary schemes. When Labour returned to power, it found itself committed to devolution and, with misgivings, published a White Paper in 1975 proposing an assembly of 142 members, with no tax-raising powers except the right to levy a surcharge on the rates. This was the basis of the Scotland and Wales Bill, defeated in the House of Commons on 22 February 1977.

As the result of a Liberal–Labour pact negotiated by James Callaghan, a new Scotland Bill was brought forward in November 1977. This was defeated in a national referendum on 1 March 1979. The nation's indifference towards devolution was demonstrated by the low turnout of 63 per cent. Although the Bill was approved by a wafer-thin majority – 77,435 out of 2,384,439 voting – it failed to reach the 40 per cent minimum approval level demanded by statute. In fact, only 33 per cent of the total electorate had approved devolution, a derisory level of support for so major a constitutional change.

This defeat also brought down the Labour government and ushered in the Thatcher era. In the period 1979 to 1997 the devolution hype, supported only by a rump of politicians and media professionals (who hoped to become bigger fish in a small pond) was maintained with difficulty. Every time the subject was mentioned in television news reports, the Royal High School building in Edinburgh, the projected home of the Parliament killed off in 1979, served as a backdrop, an icon of devolution. This was to prove ironic, in the light of the later controversy that arose with regard to housing the Parliament.

By now, however, devolution had acquired a new significance and urgency for the Scottish Left: it was seen as a means of ring-fencing Scotland against the free-market reforms of Margaret Thatcher that were sweeping across Britain and around the world. By the late 1980s, devolution had become a recipe for socialism in one country. This was signalled by the so-called 'Claim of Right for Scotland', published in July 1988 by a committee drawn from interest groups representative of corporate Scotland. On 30 March 1989 they formed themselves into the imposing-sounding Scottish Constitutional Convention.

This body was composed of representatives of the Labour and Liberal Democrat parties (which have since cohabited to create a monopoly of power under the devolution settlement), the Scottish Green Party, the Scottish Trades Union Congress (STUC), local authorities and all the usual suspects from the Scottish Left. The only non-corporatist, right-of-centre body represented was the Federation of Small Businesses: its members were subsequently rewarded for this collaboration by the devolved administration's abolition of the unified business rate and the imposition of business rates in Scotland that mushroomed to 10 per cent higher than in England.

Despite its official-sounding title, the Scottish Constitutional Convention was self-appointed, self-regarding and self-interested. Its Executive was chaired by Canon Kenyon Wright, of CND fame, and its administrative support was provided by the Labour-dominated Convention of Scottish Local Authorities (COSLA). Although the surprising return of a Conservative government at the 1992 general election disappointed its expectations, by October 1995 the Convention had drawn up a blueprint for a devolved parliament that was substantially embodied in the Scotland Act 1998.

Implementing devolution

After the Labour victory of 1997, the government lost no time in holding a referendum on devolution in Scotland. On 11 September 1997, two questions were put to the Scottish electorate: Are you in favour of a Scottish Parliament? and Should it have tax-varying powers? To the first question the reply was 'Yes' 1,775,045, 'No' 614,000; to the second, the answer was 'Yes' 1,512,889, 'No' 870,263. Yet this large vote in favour of the principle of devolution obscured the fact that the turnout, at 61.4 per cent, was actually lower than in 1979 and that only a minority of the electorate (1.7 million out of 4 million) had been moved actively to support the proposal. In the light of subsequent events, that is a caveat well worth bearing in mind: at no time in its history, even at its peak of approval, has devolution ever commanded the support of a majority of the Scottish electorate.

The Scotland Act 1998 which implemented the referendum result imported, like a plague bacillus, the 1995 recommendations of the Constitutional Convention into statute. The Parliament's membership is 129, divided between 73 directly elected MSPs and 56 'List' MSPs appointed from lists of names drawn up by party leaders. This was done in the name of Proportional Representation: its practical consequence has been that, for the first time since the 1832 Reform Act, the nominees of individuals or tiny political caucus groups sit in a parliament on British soil. When 56 members out of 129 have not been directly elected, have no constituents and, therefore, no account-ability, democracy becomes a travesty.

Nor does the Parliament have a revising chamber – another crucial flaw. Early criticism was countered by the claim that the Parliament's uniquely powerful committee system would be an adequate compensation. At the first test – the Rural Development Committee's emphatic rejection of Lord Watson's Bill to ban hunting – the system crumbled, as bigoted urban MSPs forced through the legislation. That pattern has since been repeated: nobody talks seriously now about a mighty committee system at Holyrood.

The chief flaw in the Scotland Act was one of omission: it neglected, quite deliberately, to make any provision for changing the political culture of admissions to candidature for the Parliament. During the 25-year devolution hype the vision had been promoted of a Scottish Parliament drawing upon the talent of the nation in a way that Westminster never had, of dedicated professionals from all walks of life bringing a wealth of experience to the new legislature and devoting it to the common good. The reality was that the party machines kept a stranglehold upon selection of candidates both for direct election and List MSPs. Although a handful of inde-pendent candidates have succeeded in bucking this trend, on issues such as local hospitals or pensioners' interests, the mainstream MSPs are party hacks.

Since the prevailing political culture in Scotland is machine politics based on the public sector, that is the interest group that dominates Holyrood. At the first election to the new parliament in 1999, just three categories of public-sector dependants enjoyed an absolute majority: former councillors and local government employees (50), trade union activists (nine) and tribunes drawn from the foothills of the state education system (six). With them they brought their oppressive culture of political correctness and antipathy to private enterprise: contrast the number of times the word 'inclusion' has been uttered in deliberations at Holyrood with the infrequent employment of the term 'enterprise'.

The devolved Scottish economy

Under this regime it is unsurprising that business rates rose to 10 per cent above the English level and that the Scottish economy slumped. In 2003 and 2004 Scotland had a growth rate of just 1.8 per cent, compared with 2.8 per cent and 3.2 per cent for the UK. In early 2005 the Scottish Parliament's own research department published figures showing very few small Scottish firms growing into higher-value businesses, with only 12 firms having a value of between £250m and £1bn, compared with 221 in the UK. From 1997 to 2003, the total increase in business stock in Scotland was only 4.7 per cent, but 10 per cent across the UK. Apart from feral business rates, other ideologically rooted obstacles to private enterprise could be identified. For example, medium-sized companies paid an average £6,815 per year in water charges in Scotland, compared with £2,345 in Wales: water in Scotland remains in public ownership, unlike south of the border, on the insistence of the Leftist consensus at Holyrood.

During the first quarter of 2005 Scotland's economy

showed zero growth, while the UK expanded by 0.4 per cent; Scottish GDP rose 2 per cent, compared with 2.7 per cent across the UK. Since 1997, around 100,000 manufacturing jobs have been lost in Scotland. In 2004 manufactured exports fell by £550m to £14.8bn in value, the lowest return for 10 years. Since the inception of the Scottish Parliament in 1999 the value of exports has slumped by more than a quarter. The supposedly cutting-edge Silicon Glen saw output fall in 2004 from £6.9bn to £6.2bn. The people who now run Scotland used to make a fetish of manufacturing industry and opposed tooth-and-nail the closure of such rust-bucket plants as Ravenscraig and Gartcosh. Today, they are too hostile to capitalism, or too preoccupied with jejune projects of political correctness, to create a climate of enterprise.

The Holyrood economy is rooted elsewhere. A recent statement by the chairman of Scottish Enterprise revealed that the public sector now accounts for 74 per cent of the economy of Ayrshire. Further investigations showed that in the area served by the Argyll and Clyde health board it is as high as 76 per cent. For Scotland as a whole, the figure is 55 per cent, compared with 40 per cent in England. Private enterprise is a minority element in Scotland's economic base: that amounts to a Soviet command economy. Of the Scottish workforce, 23 per cent is employed in the public sector. Local authorities now dispose of £8bn a year. When Gordon Brown indulged in his 2002 public-spending orgy, the Scottish education budget was increased by 14 per cent (for no corresponding improvement in pupil literacy or numeracy) and the health budget by £1.5bn (ditto, waiting times). The Scottish budget, which was around £15bn when Labour came to power, now stands at £24bn and is headed for £30bn by 2008. Thereafter it will decline: what will happen then? Holyrood has willingly presided over the nationalization of employment, but who will pay the piper when it all goes pear-shaped?

Scotland's public life infantilized

Yet Holyrood's free-spending ways have not bought it popularity. At the second Scottish elections in 2003 the majority of the electorate – 51 per cent – abstained. For a supposedly longed-for legislature, just four years into its existence, this was an extraordinary rebuff. Westminster, after centuries of rule, has never been so thoroughly repudiated at a general election. Holyrood has lost its mandate. The cause of this alienation, after taking into account the fact, noted above, that a majority of the electorate has never actually endorsed it, is the buffoonery that has become the hallmark of the Scottish Parliament. From its inception, Holyrood has been marked by an immaturity that is unique in the national assembly of a developed European nation. Devolution has generated infantilism in Scottish public life.

This has manifested itself even at the initial phase of MSPs being sworn in, with clenched-fist salutes and childishly subversive messages inked on the palms of hands. The word most promiscuously employed at Holyrood is 'ban', as MSPs – 56 of them not even directly elected – assert themselves by prohibiting the activities of their fellow citizens. They have even enacted a statute banning fur-farming, despite the fact that, at the committee stage of the Bill, MSPs discovered there were no fur farms in Scotland. Perhaps due to the local authority background of so many MSPs, Holyrood has preoccupied itself with trivial issues that would scarcely even merit the attention of town-hall politicians. Hence the Churchillian debate on the Dog Fouling (Scotland) Bill, or that majestic statute the Breastfeeding, etc. (Scotland) Act 2005.

The conduct of MSPs has been characterized by an obsession with political correctness, married to a totalitarian impulse to impose their own will and prejudices upon the nation. It is the classic profile of beggars on horseback – the dictatorial conduct of inadequate people who, in a truly sophisticated body politic, would hardly qualify as parliamentary janitors.

A knee-jerk prejudice against the aristocratic image of men in white stocks and red coats (actually hunt servants) inspired support for the first private member's Bill, banning fox-hunting. This measure damaged rural culture, ecology, sociability and employment. Yet it was forced through by a parliament supposedly devoted to the interests of all Scots, from motives of class warfare. Was there no more urgent issue demanding the attention of new legislators? The MSP who initiated this legislation and who was also the minister for tourism, is now in prison for fire-raising in an hotel. What does that tell us about the calibre of MSPs?

The abolition of feudalism – a very expensive reconfiguration of the entire conveyancing system – was motivated by no more sophisticated consideration than the emotive resonance of the term 'feudal', despite the fact that it had fewer oppressive connotations in Scotland than elsewhere, since serfdom had been abolished by the Scottish courts as early as 1364. Extravagant Land 'Reform' measures with confiscatory provisions against private property have been introduced, motivated by a grudge romanticism inspiring 'revenge' for the nineteenth-century Highland Clearances. The Parliament is suffering from legislative diarrhoea. During its first session, from 1999 to 2003, it passed 62 Acts. At the time of writing, during its second session, it has passed a further 27, with 14 more being processed. That makes more than 100 statutes in five years, for a nation of just five million people. This is over-government at its worst.

The extent to which membership of a legislative body had gone to the heads of MSPs was demonstrated very early in the Parliament's existence. Considering that its mandate was not as strong as it pretended, the concern of the new parliament should have been to win the confidence of the public by acting responsibly and avoiding unnecessary controversy. Instead, it provoked a confrontation with public opinion when Wendy Alexander, then Communities Minister, proposed the abolition of Section 2a (popularly known as 'Section 28', from the corresponding English legislation) of the Local Government Act 1986, which prohibited the promotion of homosexuality in schools. In an independent referendum in which more than a third of the electorate participated, 87 per cent voted against repeal of the clause. MSPs responded by denouncing their own electors as 'bigots' and then voted 99–17 against the known wishes of the public.

That was the historic moment at which the electorate parted company with the Parliament. It has never regained public confidence, as the 51 per cent abstention at the 2003 elections demonstrated. A further cause of disenchantment was the notorious fiasco of the Holyrood Parliament building. First Minister Donald Dewar railroaded it through, with the help of a committee of six yes-men (one of them broadcaster Kirsty Wark), promising it would cost between £10m and £40m. The bill currently stands at £431m, but there may be further expense when final accounts are presented. The public who had visited an exhibition of the short-listed designs had voted for a rival concept but, in the grand tradition of devolved 'consultations', their opinion was ignored.

MSPs have also alienated the public by their feathering of their own nests. As early as 2002 they increased their salaries by 14 per cent, in the same month that nurses were awarded 4 per cent; today, taking salaries and allowances together, MSPs earn more than £100,000 a year for a notoriously short working week and lengthy holidays. The financial malfeasance that forced the resignation of Henry McLeish, the second First Minister, exposed a culture of shameless, self-seeking greed at the public expense.

What is to be done?

Devolution has been a disaster for Scotland. It survives chiefly through the fatalistic mantra 'Devolution is here to stay'. Why? It is damaging Scotland deeply, so it must either be reformed or abolished. The immediate problem is that the sole political organization not belonging to the big-government consensus – the Scottish Conservative Party – has gone native. The Scottish Tories are in the extraordinary position of having been proved right – a rare experience for politicians – in their opposition to devolution, but feeling ashamed of it. Chastened by their 1997 defeat, they have lost no opportunity of proving themselves collaborators with the new order. This Vichy mentality has even led them increasingly to espouse the cause of 'full fiscal autonomy', i.e. giving the spendthrift incompetents at Holyrood unrestricted control of all revenue raised in Scotland.

The consequences for business and wealth-creation do not bear thinking about. Even Scottish Labour has not taken so ambitious a stance. The Tories do so on the specious grounds that it would make Holyrood more 'accountable'. In the way that local government is accountable, do they mean? This insane policy ignores the political demography of Scotland. Of an electorate of almost 4 million, only 2.3 million pay taxes. A massive 21.6 per cent of people of working age are claiming a key benefit or receiving a tax credit. As already noted, 23 per cent of the workforce is in the public sector, where increased taxation will always be neutralized by pay increases. Where is the constituency there for fiscal responsibility? Turn on the spigot and lie under it open-mouthed, is the majority instinct.

For those who desire to see Scotland join the free-enterprise nations of the world and cast off the yoke of dependency, devolution is the dragon that must be slain. It may be politically prudent to canvass reform before abolition. Such proposals should include the abolition of List MSPs; a reduction in the number of members to around 106, in harmony with the recent cut in MPs; and the creation of a revising chamber to moderate the more outrageous legislative initiatives of the Parliament. Any Holyrood election with a turnout below 50 per cent should be invalidated and re-run. If the electors decide to stay at home even on the second poll, that would be a satisfactory way of putting a parliament that no longer commands public confidence into mothballs, on the Stormont model, for four years until further elections fall due.

Reformers should also consider holding a second, confirmatory referendum on the existence of the Parliament. Even if a canny Scottish instinct to hold onto any possession, however shabby, prompted another Yes vote, the knowledge that a plebiscite was pending would concentrate MSPs' minds and perhaps make them address issues of substance rather than treating the Parliament as a forum for self-indulgence. An alternative reform that has been suggested is to make MSPs and MPs the same people, sitting at Holyrood three days a week and at Westminster on one day set aside for Scottish business on reserved matters. That would effectively remove a superfluous tier of government and reduce the salary costs of members, besides finally resolving the West Lothian question.

All of these options would require Westminster legislation. Yet it is at Westminster that the devolution problem must finally be confronted, under the next Conservative government. Any Tory administration that allowed itself to be persuaded that full fiscal autonomy for Scotland is a solution would be gravely deluded. The existence of a Conservative government at Westminster in tandem with a Labour administration at Holyrood – until recently regarded as so hypothetical that consideration of its implications could be deferred indefinitely – will pose enormous difficulties.

Holyrood has control of every policy area apart from social security, defence, foreign affairs and macroeconomics. Two increasingly diverging economies and societies would put grave strain on the Union. No federal solution is possible, since the north-east of England threw out devolution in a referendum and the other regions regard it with evident hostility. It is no longer beyond the bounds of possibility that, at some point in the future, a UK Conservative government would be compelled by the tensions between Westminster and Holyrood to present the Scottish electorate with a new referendum, offering a choice between the pre-1998 settlement and independence, with unworkable devolution no longer an option.

The extent to which devolution is still uncharted territory has been glossed over by the coincidence of Labour government at both Westminster and Holyrood since its inception. Even that relative compatibility (although Holyrood is Old Labour) has not protected Scotland from the ravages inflicted upon it by childish politicians playing in a legislative sandpit. Yet the original purpose of devolution, after 1979, was to preserve Scotland as a pre-Thatcherite theme park for dinosaurs and the advent of a UK Conservative government would see that function kicking in. The assumptions of the 'progressive consensus' north of the border are those of an unreconstructed socialism whose illusions would nowadays be laughed to scorn by the meanest Albanian peasant; yet they are axiomatic around the dinner tables of the highly salaried public-sector nomenklatura in Scotland.

If devolution is not remodelled or repealed, the tragic consequence will be a slow death for Scotland. At least in its present form, it must not be here to stay.

*   *   *

Gerald Warner, OStJ, MA, FSAScot, is one of Scotland's most outstanding writers and columnists. Publications include *Homelands of the Clans* (1980); *Being of Sound Mind* (1980); *Tales of the Scottish Highlands* (1982); *Conquering by Degrees* (1985) and *The Scottish Tory Party: A History* (1988). He has been a blistering critic of devolution since the Parliament was opened.

ALAN COCHRANE

6

Looking to a new
political alignment

1. A story of 'success'

The Scottish Parliament is a success. There, I've said it.

There can no longer be any doubt. Scotland's new, controversial and ferociously expensive democratic institution has been a triumph. But it is a triumph due to a flawed prospectus, a prescription for Scotland based more on a visceral dislike of something that the Scots believed had been imposed upon them – a middle-class English woman called Margaret Thatcher and her Mr Pooter-like successor, John Major – than for any aching desire for devolution.

However, to return to my opening statement, the plain fact is that the building at the foot of the Royal Mile has captured the public's imagination in a way I find remarkable. This is all the more so considering the controversy surrounding its construction.

Of course, one reason why more than 100,000 have visited the Holyrood building since it finally opened for business in autumn 2004 may well be the curiosity of taxpayers, keen – desperate even – to see where all of their money went.

But that isn't the only reason. They go there, in their droves, in their church groups, in their classrooms, in their

OAP associations, to see what has become known, simply, as 'The Parliament'.

It was Sir Malcolm Rifkind who first explained the distinction to me. 'Westminster is', he said, 'in the minds of the public, plain "parliament". Just as it has always been. But Holyrood has become "the Parliament".' This from the MP for Kensington and Chelsea who preferred eight years in the political wilderness, rather than chance his arm in the devolution lists.

But 'the Parliament' has become so quickly the focus of Scotland's democracy it almost gives the lie, superficially at least, to Enoch Powell's great maxim that 'power devolved is power retained'. Rightly or wrongly the perception of what a government can or cannot do has come to be based on what devolution – or, specifically, what the Scottish Executive and the Scottish Parliament – can do.

And this is why, I suspect, so many people come to Holyrood every day to see what goes on and why, as I once overheard a tour guide say to a group of visitors as she ushered them into the parliamentary chamber, 'Now let us go and see the seat of Scottish democracy.'

Never mind that MSPs meet in plenary for only nine hours a week, not counting their 14-week holiday. There was not a trace of irony in her voice.

I found it an incredible statement. That it was entirely wrong goes without saying. But that was what a perfectly ordinary and educated Edinburgh lady said to her audience. As such it was a sign of how much the idea of the Scottish Parliament as a 'good thing' has permeated official Scottish thinking. It also shows how readily much of the Scottish public has accepted it – despite its stunning deficiencies. Devolution and 'the Parliament' are now the status quo. And devolutionists are probably correct in their belief that another referendum would probably produce another big 'Yes' vote.

How did we get here? A devo-enthusiast would say that

such was the demand, fervour even, for devolution that it was inevitable it would quickly enter the public mind as a natural way of doing things.

Personally, I think it was more likely the fevered demand for devolution amongst the bulk of Scotland's permanently Left-leaning establishment ensured, if not its success, then at least the almost universal *acceptance* of devolution.

They at least knew what they were about. The majority of the population wanted shot of the Tories. That was clear. But Labour and Liberal Democrats were playing a new tune, a distinctly Scottish tune that suggested something that wasn't a whole lot different from what the (by then Jim Sillars-less) nationalists were also suggesting.

It proved a heady brew. However, no more than 42 per cent of those eligible to vote opted for it – the actual result of the 1997 referendum was only slightly more than was required in the 1978 Cunningham amendment. But it was still enough to be hailed as a significant victory. And it was an elixir so powerful that, six years after first supping it, most Scots regard as bonkers people like me who would unravel the lot and return to Westminster rule tomorrow.

My principal worry about the *apparent* success – widespread acceptance is probably the more correct description – of devolution is not, however, concerned with people like me. Those of my generation have pre-Holyrood memories. We remember a Scotland when it was not cluttered with layer upon layer of government and attendant bureaucracies. We can remember life without 'the Parliament'.

Unfortunately for them and, I suspect, the future of this country, there are generations now arising that have no such memory. I refer to the schoolchildren ushered in their countless numbers round Holyrood every day. For them, this is, as that tour guide said, 'the seat of Scotland's democracy', for the simple reason that they know no other.

How many, I wonder, either before or after their trip to Holyrood, sit down to a lesson about how it is but one of Scotland's parliaments and that the other, at Westminster, is still the centre of power in this still United Kingdom? How many are left only with the firm impression that the Scottish Parliament is 'it'? Of course let us expose our children to the workings of our democratic institutions. But so insular has devolution made us that, even for non-nationalists, Holyrood has become the be-all to end-all.

Does the Hansard Society, for instance, or any of the other burgeoning and worthy think-tanks that litter Scottish public life at present, ever consider spending their apparently limit-less cash on spreading the real message of democracy in Scot-land – that Scotland and Scots have a proud record of success at that seemingly far-off parliament on the banks of Thames? That is the real seat of Britain's and Scotland's democracy. The two are indivisible.

2. Creeping nationalism

Compare the following two statements, uttered in the run-up to the 1997 general election and the subsequent referendum on the Scottish Parliament.

John Major: With devolution, the Scots will be sleep-walking towards independence.
George (now Lord) Robertson: Devolution will kill the Scottish National Party stone dead.

At first glance it would appear that the crystal-ball gazing of the former Secretary of State for Scotland was more accurate than that of the former Prime Minister. After all, the nation-alist share of the vote has gone down consistently since devolution – during which the SNP helped secure a 'Yes, Yes' verdict – and has never reached the giddy heights of 30 per cent it achieved in 1974.

Indeed, the SNP has looked to be in the doldrums for much of the post-devolution period. Alex Salmond, its leader on Devolution Day, looked ill-at-ease in the new parliament. Having acted in concert with the Labour and Liberal Democrat leaders, Donald Dewar and Jim Wallace, in the referendum campaign, old hard-man Salmond found it harder still to adapt to the supposedly less-confrontational ways of doing things. Although he could never, ever, admit to it, there was little doubt that Mr Salmond found the bear-pit atmosphere of the House of Commons much more congenial to his way of politicking than the supposedly touchy-feely new parliament in Edinburgh.

This consensual approach to what is, after all, a tough old game was always doomed to fail and fail, thank goodness, it did, and quickly. Politics is a confrontational business, and the voter is best served when the various protagonists step up to the mark and slug it out. The quaint notion that the Consultative Steering Group (CSG) had of a 'love-thy-neighbour', 'after-you-Claude' assembly where everything was sweetness and light was so much baloney.

The Scottish Parliament did become a shouting match. Voices were raised continuously. People did get thrown out. Partisanship came home to rule, as it was always bound to do. And the SNP were well to the fore in bringing an end to any consensus, almost before it had begun. However, the question remained – not just for their activists and members, but also for the voters at large – had devolution shot the Nats' fox? Wasn't it enough, now, to have that impressive phalanx of powers over almost everything barring defence, foreign affairs and terrorism, without having to go the whole hog of breaking up the United Kingdom?

What need was there for a party that was not content to have a parliament with all of these powers but which wanted more, more and yet more before that parliament had proved that it could wisely use the ones it already had?

George Robertson appeared to have got it right, especially after Mr Salmond beetled off back to Westminster, citing ten years as leader as being enough, and leaving the relatively mild-mannered but still-passionate nationalist, John Swinney, to take over the reins. His tenure saw the forced departure of Henry McLeish as First Minister, over an expenses muddle, although it was David McLetchie, the Tory leader, who won the plaudits for that assassination. The same Mr McLetchie resigned in November 2005, ironically, over his own expenses muddle.

However, the travails of the Labour Party did not seem to bring tangible benefit for the SNP and their vote plummeted in the 2004 Euro-elections to such an extent that Mr Swinney threw in the towel, forcing Mr Salmond to take over once more as 'convenor', with his protégée, Nicola Sturgeon, becoming leader in the Scottish Parliament. Although a lively debater, with an eye always on the main chance, Ms Sturgeon has done a competent but not brilliant job as Leader of the Opposition.

All of which, taken together, suggests again that Lord Robertson had hit the nail on the head. The trouble with this verdict, however, is that it ignores the active role that his very own Labour Party – or at least the First Minister, Jack McConnell – took in playing the nationalist card and, who knows, bringing John Major's dire prediction to fruition.

Mr McConnell had come to power, pledging 'to do less, better' and with a reputation of having good relations with Scotland's media. On the first, it soon proved that not only did he have no real vision for a future Scotland, but he had precious little by way of policies, either – save for aping Tony

Blair in a crackdown on anti-social behaviour and to ban smoking in public places.

On the second of his supposed strong points – his 'touch' for relations with the press – he quickly came a cropper over two ludicrous incidents that earned him huge amounts of bad publicity. The first was when he togged himself up in a pin-stripe kilt while in New York – earning national and international ignominy. The second, when he decided to attend a golf dinner rather than the D-Day celebrations in Normandy, showed a bemused nation that he simply wasn't up to the job. The fact that he recanted when driven to do so by the Scottish press did not save his reputation but it soured his relations, irreparably, with the Fourth Estate.

It was following this imbroglio – and the pasting he'd had from the media – that saw him branch out into new and uncharted waters, forging his own Scottish 'foreign' policy, one that to all intents and purposes he pursues independently not just of Whitehall but of the rest of the ministers in the Scottish Executive.

It is true that tentative steps had been taken in this direction by both his predecessors, Donald Dewar and Henry McLeish. However, under McConnell it has become an art form. Always a keen European, he had been given responsibility for Scotland's relations with Europe under both Dewar and McLeish, and this clearly stood him in good stead when he became First Minister. He was elected chairman of the Regional Assemblies of the EU – RegLeg for short. What this organization does, or exists for, other than to allow the heads of Europe's state-lets to strut their stuff on provincial stages, is a mystery to most people. But it does appear to meet regularly and require Mr McConnell's attendance at all times.

Then there are foreign postings. Scotland already has diplomatic representation, at First Secretary level, in the

Washington and Beijing embassies and there are plans for more such posts, ostensibly to deal with matters of education (selling Scottish universities) and trade. There is also a Scottish Executive outpost, dealing with relations with the EU, in Brussels. Why? I have not the slightest idea. But every time such an appointment is announced, there are whoops of joy from the SNP who would, of course, pepper the world with Scottish embassies.

Then there is Tartan Day. It was dreamed up initially by Trent Lott, the Republican US senator of Scots extraction, to commemorate the 1320 signing of the Scottish Declaration of Independence, on which many Americans say their version of UDI was based. Mr McLeish was the first First Minister to attend. But his modest entourage now looks puny alongside the phalanx of hangers-on and apparatchiks who accompany Mr McConnell. For those who are keen on feasts of Tartanalia, this celebration is a must. For others it has become cringe-making.

Next up was the McConnell Mission to Malawi, where the First Minister decided to forge a unique and special relationship with that poverty-stricken African country whose long associations with Scotland appear to have done it not one whit of good. But off Jack went, accompanied by an uncritical press pack, to pledge undying friendship and a wee bit of money for that benighted and corruption-ridden land.

He was barely back from sub-Saharan Africa before he was in the throes of the G8 summit at Gleneagles Hotel in Perthshire. This was, McConnell reckoned, another heaven-sent opportunity to put Scotland and himself on the world map. He even invented, or had invented for him, a new slogan specially for the summit. Scotland, banners everywhere told everyone, was 'the best small country in the world'. Then Mr McConnell lined himself up with the Make Poverty History marchers and insisted that the summit *must* do something about world, and especially, African poverty. In spite of his posturing and grandstanding, all he managed to grab for himself was a sort of maitre d' role at the conference, meeting and greeting the G8 leaders as they flew into Scotland. He also wangled a seat for himself at the top table – but only for lunch and dinner. The big boys excluded him from the serious talking.

When the terrorist atrocities in London all but wrecked the summit's proceedings, Mr McConnell insisted that he should issue a message of condolence to Londoners, as if the intensely moving statement from Britain's prime minister had not been enough.

The summer over, Mr McConnell was back on foreign affairs duties once more – prompting John Reid, the defence secretary, on a rare visit to the Scottish Parliament, to quip: 'That's Jack for you. If he's not in Malawi, he's in New York.' Mr McConnell staged a week-long visit to the USA and Canada, visiting and seeking the support of – we're told – the Scottish Diaspora, including one Donald Trump, alongside whom Mr McConnell had himself photographed.

In Edinburgh there was more Malawi business to conduct, with a special conference on the urgent needs of that country. This was attended by its president, as well as by Princess Anne, the Princess Royal, and a host of international donors and aid experts.

Then, in mid November, it was off to Munich for two days of RegLeg business . . . not bad for a politician whose duties and responsibilities are supposed to *exclude* foreign affairs. There is not a shred of doubt that what they see as unnecessary gallivanting irks the hell out of Scottish Westminster-based politicians. But there is not a thing they can do about it. When it comes to what's best for Scotland, Mr McConnell can do pretty much what he likes. If he thinks Scotland's best interests are served by offering aid packages to starving

Africans or hob-nobbing with regional bigwigs in Europe's best hotels, then that's entirely a matter for him.

However, it is not merely in relation to his prodigious clocking up of Air Miles that Mr McConnell is in danger of proving John Major right. In his domestic affairs, too, he is pushing hard at the boundaries of the so-called devolution 'settlement'. It has always been the case that Scottish politicians wish to go the 'Scottish way' on policy, even if they know – as in education and health – that they'd be better off following the examples set in both fields south of the border. But Mr McConnell has gone one step further in several avenues of government policy, and specifically in aspects of our everyday life that are supposed to be 'reserved' to Westminster. Mr McConnell may well pay lip service to the Union. But he does appear to wish to have it both ways on a range of issues.

Take immigration. The United Kingdom government generally feels that we need to cut back on the number of immigrants coming into this country. Mr McConnell, however, is worried that Scotland's ageing population is shrinking at an alarming rate and that we desperately need new blood in the shape of more skilled migrants. To this end he launched his Fresh Talent initiative which, on the one hand allows university graduates to stay on longer in Scotland than they would in other parts of the UK, and on the other seeks to get a special deal for immigrants to Scotland. Fearful that such people would simply hop on the first train to London, where they're generally not wanted, the Home Office is resisting Mr McConnell's blandishments. For his part, however, the First Minister, cheered on by the SNP, Greens and Socialists, continues to insist that Scotland needs to be treated as a special – and separate – case.

The situation on asylum seekers is similar. Here, Mr McConnell has been goaded by the Greens and Socialists about the 'brutal dawn raids' which see failed asylum seekers and their families thrown out of Britain and has promised – cravenly in the eyes of many Westminster-based Labour politicians – to seek a 'protocol' from the Home Office that would permit such asylum seekers to be treated differently in Scotland than they would be in the rest of the United Kingdom. But the First Minister has been as unsuccessful on this front as he is with the immigration question. However, the point is not being missed – Jack McConnell wants Scotland to be significantly different from the rest of the UK. Other than for securing cheap headlines why is he behaving like this?

On a minor note, but still in an attempt to make UK legislation dance to a devolved tune, Mr McConnell tried to have the Home Office amend the legislation covering the sale and use of airguns following the murder of a Glasgow toddler by a drug addict armed with an air rifle. As in so much of his negotiations with that Whitehall department, he failed as much because ministers and officials there guard jealously their right to make law for the whole of the UK as because of their view that Mr McConnell's demands for draconian curbs were out of all proportion to the problem. They were also a knee-jerk reaction to lurid tabloid headlines.

Individually, these attempts to unsettle the so-called devolution settlement may not amount to much. But taken together they represent a blatant move by an opportunist politician to paint Whitehall departments as the bad guys while he portrays himself as the hero fighting Scotland's corner. It is manna from Heaven for all those who love to blame the English for Scotland's ills. Incredibly, a large proportion of Scotland's media fall for it.

Added to these pressures, there are also Mr McConnell's nudges and winks that he wouldn't mind in the least if there was a widespread debate about increasing and extending the powers of the Scottish Parliament, again providing just the ammunition the nationalists, in all their guises, desire.

What makes the situation worse is that Mr McConnell is a supposed Unionist, who supports the continued existence of the United Kingdom of Great Britain and Northern Ireland. Yet he adopts a policy of creeping nationalism. What might happen if we ever get a 'real' nationalist in Bute House?

3. A future realignment?

I cannot be the only observer of the Scottish scene to be surprised that the demarcation lines between the political parties have remained virtually intact since devolution. I had anticipated that the Scottish Parliament would, relatively swiftly, bring about a realignment on the Left, Right and centre. However, at time of writing at least there are few visible signs of anything of the kind being under way. True, there have been a couple of show trials and public rows that have seen the likes of Brian Monteith, Campbell Martin and – most significantly of all – Margo MacDonald resign and/or be booted out of their former parties. And Dennis Canavan included himself out of the Labour Party before the new parliament even got going.

But the shape and structure of the old parties remain pretty much as they've always been. The reason for this – and this is what I underestimated – can be put down in large measure to the fierce tribal loyalty that most of its members evince towards the Labour Party.

Through the most troubled of periods, including the jailing of one of its leading lights, the former minister for tourism, for attempted fire-raising in one of Edinburgh's top hotels, the death of one First Minister and the forced resignation of another, Labour has managed to remain a formidably united force. There are stresses and strains both within the Scottish party and in its relations with the party and government, nationally. But these have not been allowed to deflect it from what it sees as its main role in life – which is to govern Scotland, as it almost always has. This will to run things supersedes all else, no matter the individual differences on policy.

And it is the strength and solidity of Scottish Labour that has, in my opinion, also helped the other parties to maintain their shape. The main opposition party, the SNP, is an amalgam of various shades of political opinion, ranging from out and out socialists to old fashioned right-wing Tartan Tories, with a soggy centre of social democrat statists. They are all supposed to be united around a burning desire for independence and the break-up of the United Kingdom. But even here the water is muddied by the different approaches advocated by the different factions of the party in achieving that independence.

The Scottish Conservative and Unionist Party, to give the country's oldest political party its full title, is as united as it has always been, which means not much. Its MSPs are viewed with much scepticism by the members in the country, a fair proportion of whom – perhaps even a majority – would prefer it if the party had nothing whatsoever to do with the Scottish Parliament. However, that view will fade over time and the divisions will remain the same as they've always been in the Conservative Party – between the wets and the drys. *Plus ça change.*

The Scottish Liberal Party has benefited most from devolution and the PR system that has given it a share of government and several ministerial posts, as well as the trappings of power that the UK party can only dream of. They are opportunists *par excellence,* using pork barrel politics of the most shameful nature to benefit their own parts of the country – viz the abolition of the tolls on the Skye Bridge and the hugely expensive 'railway to nowhere' in the Borders. But as an all-things-to-all-men party, it is well-placed to mop up any deserters from the other parties.

The six Scottish Socialists face an uncertain future. They cannot seem to make up their mind between parliamentary representation and direct action. They initiate debates and do their stuff in long and boring committee meetings. But then they kick over the traces and get banned from the chamber for childish demonstrations. And then, of course, there is their penchant for getting arrested. Their former leader, Tommy Sheridan, has had his collar felt more often than any other British politician. They are arguably the parliament's least united party – a faction, within a clique, within a schism – having ousted the aforesaid Mr Sheridan as convenor but facing the prospect of seeing him survive as their sole remaining MSP after the next Holyrood elections in 2007.

The Greens, by way of contrast, may well inherit, if not the earth, then at least a share of government. Their MSPs are a disparate bunch, ranging from traditional tree huggers to gay-rights activists. But, and for reasons that are beyond me, they may well retain or even increase their seven-strong representation, especially if the ridiculously unfair party list system remains in place. This could well give them a place in a rainbow coalition or at least give them the whip hand in negotiating parliamentary deals with one or more larger parties.

And it is this uncertainty that could see the realignment for which I have been looking. Struan Stevenson, a Tory Member of the European Parliament, recently posited the idea of a Tory/SNP alliance to combat Labour's spendthrift ways. The only thing he forgot was that the SNP is much more left wing than Scottish Labour and would spend more, not less, in the public sector than does Labour at present. However, he was correct to explore the possibilities of coalitions, deals, arrangements – call them what you will. An election result, with no two parties able to command a parliamentary majority, could well provide the opportunity for MSPs to break with party loyalties and vote on grounds of conscience for individual policies on their merits.

My contention is that devolution has made the old labels redundant. Let's hear it for a realignment.

*　　　　*　　　　*

Alan Cochrane is the Scottish political correspondent for the *Daily Telegraph*.

TOM MIERS

7

A liberal state to set
Scotland free

SCOTLAND'S TROUBLES are well known. Low economic growth; poor educational attainment; a health service characterized by queues and poor disease survival rates; high welfare dependency and crime.

These problems are discussed by authors elsewhere in this book. It is enough to say here that Scotland's ambition in dealing with its problems should be boundless. Too often the defenders of the status quo quibble with the overall picture by using the excuses of detail. They say that growth rates aren't too bad when compared with the UK over certain periods, or that we cannot compare Scottish state schools fairly with international or independent rivals. Tinkering is the best we can do: EU rules would stop any radical tax changes, and our climate and geography means that health outcomes must be low and spending high.

It is time to lift up our gaze and aspire to be the best again. Instead of comparing growth rates with English regions, we should look to the dynamic economies of Estonia and the Irish Republic; to the healthcare system of Singapore or France; to the schools of South Korea or the Netherlands. And the transport network of Japan or Hong Kong.

Scots should be inspired by their own past, because it tells

us that the best is possible here. Glasgow was once the richest
city on the planet. The first mass-literate society, Scotland's
intellectual achievements were stunning, producing pioneers
in engineering, medicine, economics and philosophy way out
of proportion to its population.

It is this optimistic and ambitious approach I would like to
see rekindled in Scotland. Twentieth-century socialism caused
atrophy in many of Scotland's institutions which led to our
decline. Fortunately a new consensus is arising about the
limits of state effectiveness as a provider of services. This
presents Scotland with an opportunity to remodel the relationship between citizen and state to unleash Scots native
dynamism once again.

However, policy changes may not be enough. I also argue
that Scotland's devolved constitution entrenches poor
governance which will make reform harder and vulnerable
to regression. But the precedent of devolution presents a
second opportunity to Scotland: Scots now have the power
to order their own lives. They should use this to create a new
liberal method of government which limits the powers of the
state and entrenches the freedom of the individual to secure
a new age of enlightenment in Scotland.

The new consensus

The post-war period saw an intellectual and political triumph
of democratic socialism in Britain. The state seized ownership
and control of a huge section of the British economy that had
previously been run by voluntary institutions such as families,
companies or charities. The normal political swings between
the parties barely affected this change, until the problems
associated with state management of industries and services
became apparent after a generation.

These problems are now well understood. Government monopoly control removes competition from industries and services, and therefore the incentives to innovate, improve productivity and service quality, and reduce costs. This process stymies overall growth and prosperity.

Scottish society has atrophied along certain predictable lines. It is noticeable that those areas most controlled by the state have sunk lowest by international standards – healthcare, state education, town planning. Meanwhile, those fields of endeavour which still foster excellence in Scotland have little or nothing to do with the state – certain industries such as financial services or whisky, independent schools and popular music, for example.

The good news is that there is a growing political consensus in the UK which recognizes the limitations of state control, and the importance of reform to reintroduce competition and variety. The following quote shows how, for example, Tony Blair has accepted this:

Choice is crucial both to individual empowerment and – by enabling the consumer to move to an alternative provider where dissatisfied – to quality of service.[1]

He and others in New Labour have realized that Britain made a historic mistake in the post-war period of creating state owned monopoly providers of health and education.

They have understood we must reintroduce competition into these two industries, to benefit consumer and employee alike. To do this, we need only look at the continental example where, in most countries this mistake was never made.

---

1 *The courage of our convictions – Why reform of the public services is the route to social justice*, Tony Blair, Fabian Ideas, 603, September 2002.

Indeed, the drag on Britain's economy caused by its unproductive public sector is one of the main reasons why the UK's overall performance has not exceeded the Continental economies by more than it has. The truth is that, although the redistribution of wealth in these countries is usually more extensive than in the UK, there is no 'public' sector in the way we understand it to act as a dead weight on their economies.

There is of course a large range of health and education systems across Europe and the developed world, involving different patterns of ownership, different models of patient/parent control, and different ways of financing them. But while the state *funds* them it does not *run* them. There is competition by example or directly, because variety is encouraged and entrenched.

A promising example which may be applicable to Scotland is the recent reforms of both health and education services in Sweden. This shows that change can be rapid and effective. It is nonsense to point to special circumstances in Scotland. Sweden's geographical, demographic and climatic problems mirror Scotland's, but on a larger scale.

Indeed, the thrust of New Labour's reforms in England of health and education is very reminiscent of the Swedish experience, in that their focus is on introducing consumer choice and leaving intact the taxpayer-funded payment system. The obvious aim is to reap maximum benefit with minimum upheaval. As such the reforms are flawed. But they do at least put flesh on the new consensus.

As a result the logic of devolution will expose the performance of the retrograde Scottish system within a few years (indeed it is already beginning to do so). This, combined with the political consensus that is forming means that similar reforms are inevitable here. The Conservatives and the Labour leadership are now wholly committed to this agenda. The Liberal Democrats and the SNP both host cliques that subscribe to it, and these are growing in influence, though not yet leading their parties.

The next debate

The intellectual case that the state should not run services has now been largely won. It is now a matter of time, political tactics and implementation before Scotland enjoys the bounty of this revolution.[2]

This presents a further opportunity here. The challenge now is for liberals to look beyond public sector reform, and shift the debate further by taking the argument to its logical conclusion.

A liberal ideal is a society where people, or at least small groups such as families and neighbourhoods, are self-reliant and don't need the state to supply the necessities of life.

This need not seem so far-fetched when you consider what complex fields of life are already left to the individual with minimal government intervention, such as the supply and purchase of food, or the manufacture, sale, maintenance and insurance of motor cars.

---

2   It is true that it has proved surprisingly difficult to sell this 'choice agenda' as it is known to the public. Specious counter-arguments like 'we must have good local schools' abound. The answer may be to point to the likely *results* of competition, not the attractions of the process. The truth is that some people don't feel comfortable exercising choice. But most people don't have to for competition to work and standards to rise everywhere. Highlighting the *results* of competition – no waiting lists, good local schools, etc. – is probably more effective than pointing out the attractions of parental or patient choice. That canny political operator Tony Blair seems to have grasped this, even to the extent of changing the language of the debate – talking about 'contestability' instead of competition. Though his *fin de siècle* troubles at the time of writing may thwart even him.

In both these industries, while the state sets certain standards (such as compulsory motor insurance, or welfare benefits to ensure that the poorest can afford food), individuals are left to operate within markets where competition on price as well as quality is the norm, and new developments and innovation are continual and commonplace. There is now no reason why this model should not be extended to all those industries and services currently still managed by the state, bar defence and the justice system.

We have seen how the consensus has changed to encourage schools and hospitals to compete on quality, with the state as funder and access 'free at the point of delivery'. The weakness of this voucher-based model is that its lacks scope for competition on *price*, so central in other industries. So, while there is room for quality to improve, prices are not given the chance to fall – reducing the potential benefits from market-based reforms in these industries.

So the next step is to allow providers to compete on price by giving cash to citizens and allowing them to shop around on the understanding that, as with motor insurance, health insurance and education for children is compulsory. The cash amount would be based on an average of the price of such services, with citizens allowed to keep any surplus gained from finding the best deal. As competition drove down prices as well as improving standards, this average, and therefore the amount spent by the nation on health and education, could fall. Equally, if prices *rose* to accommodate, for example, new technologies, higher life expectancy or just a preference for more health and education services, the average, and therefore the total amount would also rise. Either way, the market mechanism would find the right level of spending for both health and education, a level currently guessed at by the crude and uncertain political process.

As people became more used to exercising these important

choices the compulsory element could be removed. The prize would be a return to a liberal society where 90 per cent are responsible enough to look after their own needs, leaving care of the weakest well within the capabilities and resources of the voluntary sector.

The economic advantages of such a progression are obvious. A price-as-well-as-quality market in health and education would lead to a far more efficient allocation of resources, with the potential for lower taxes, smaller government bureaucracy, and much higher productivity in these sectors, all leading to higher economic growth.

Indeed, there is no reason why these principles should not be applied to other areas where the state is now dominant. We already enjoy the power to use part of our tax liability to invest in the pension scheme of our choice, by opting out of the State Earnings Related Pension Scheme (SERPS). The logic of this precedent, and the potential developments in health and education discussed above, is to extend our competitive, price-sensitive model to welfare. We currently have a benefit-based welfare regime, with its exposure to expensive bureaucracy and claimant abuse. It encourages dependency and the breakdown of families and neighbourliness, with serious implications for levels of crime. Instead, citizens should simply be required to buy pension provision and insurance against unemployment, disability and other 'entitling' mishaps from private providers out of their cash entitlement which again would vary with average prices. Private insurers are much more effective at detecting fraudulent claims and incentivizing behaviour designed to keep premiums down – their livelihoods depend on it.

To conclude, this cash entitlement would be funded as now by taxation, but its use decided on by the individual to buy those services and social security currently supplied by the state from a more productive private sector: healthcare, education, a pension and insurance against unemployment and other mishaps.

To begin with, it would be compulsory to buy each element of the range, but with individual discretion on both the provider and the balance of spending on each. As society returned to more self-reliance over time, the element of compulsion could be removed, and the overall entitlement allowed to decline.

The constitution of socialism

As I have argued, the growing political consensus that government makes a poor provider of public services points to an opportunity for a future liberal society where individuals purchase social security and 'public services' in the market place. This has enormously beneficial potential for the quality of these services, economic and social performance, and therefore the welfare of our people.

However, arguing for policy reform of this kind is not enough. The reason that the consensus has changed is not because of a philosophical conversion of our governing class, but because the failure of the socialist model became so manifest even to Labour politicians like Tony Blair. The next section of this chapter argues that our constitution has developed in a way that makes socialism pretty much inevitable, in the sense that there exist mechanisms whose bias is constantly towards more government control and higher taxes. To reverse this trend even temporarily takes enormous political upheaval usually provoked by crisis, such as the 1970s industrial crisis which provoked the Thatcher reforms and the manifest failures in health and education which caused the Blair government to change course.

The danger exists, therefore, that liberal reform will prove short-lived and incomplete, and the grind back to socialism and eventual crisis will repeat itself.

To encourage and safeguard a liberal society, therefore, we must understand how our method of government became so prone to socialism, and thus attempt to redress the balance.

The twentieth century was the age of socialism. All Western societies saw an enormous increase in state power as socialism became the dominant intellectual creed, and democracy its tool to redistribute resources of all kinds.

The struggles against Nazism and then Communism juxtaposed the Western democracies as beacons of liberalism. The democracies have indeed avoided the excesses of arbitrary dictatorship until now. But the last 100 years nonetheless saw an enormous increase in the economic power of the state in Britain and elsewhere. More recently we have witnessed worrying erosions of civil liberties as well.

Graph 1 shows the increase in taxation as a proportion of GDP in the major Western-style democracies.

This represents a massive exercise in the redistribution of wealth in these countries. While patterns of spending have varied enormously, as we have seen the great bulk of it has been on various forms of welfare, in the form of direct benefits payments or free healthcare, education and other services.

This represents a triumph for the socialist ideal. In an attempt to cure the social problems associated with the Industrial Revolution, governments have succeeded in extending their power deep into the economic and social lives of their citizens.

Thus has the work of seventeenth-, eighteenth- and nineteenth-century liberalism in countries such as Britain and the USA been undermined. It is as if, having finally shackled the monster of government absolutism after 300 years of struggle, it was suddenly released again. How did this happen?

Graph 1: Government expenditure as percentage of GDP

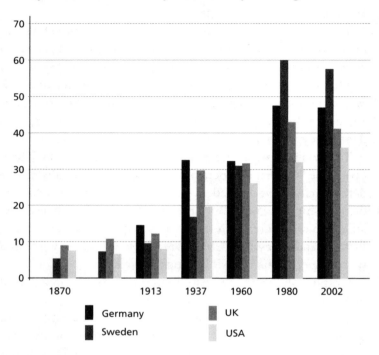

Germany   UK
Sweden   USA

The dynamic of democracy

Since the rise of socialism coincides with the advent of democracy in these states, it is reasonable to suppose that the two are connected.

Without going into a lengthy political and historical discourse, it is worth pointing to three dynamics which seem to characterize modern political economy.

1. Democratic incentives towards redistribution

As long as income inequality exists, there is usually political advantage to be gained in a democracy from providing benefits to the majority at the expense of the rest. This is why taxes in democracies tend towards 50 per cent of GDP (see Graph 1). But they cannot go above 50 per cent for long, because then the dynamic reverses, and the taxed minority becomes a majority (see the case of Sweden in Graph 1).

Politicians also seek to provide their constituents with specific benefits, the costs of which are diffused and barely noticed by those paying them.

2. Democratic incentives towards action

Modern democracies have seen their political classes becoming increasingly professional. Today, politicians in Britain and elsewhere often spend their whole career in politics. Their *raison d'être* is to implement law and regulation. Whether they are Brussels Commissioners, town councillors or Members of the Scottish Parliament, the overwhelming pressure is to be seen to legislate to prove their usefulness to their electors. They even agitate for more time and resources (in terms of money and personnel) to facilitate this.

3. The legitimatization of democracy

Rule by a popular or elected majority has now acquired a legitimacy of its own. We are constantly hearing our elected politicians invoking a popular or electoral 'mandate' for action. Unelected bodies are often denigrated for impeding the 'democratic will'. It is as if a majority, however small, in an elected chamber or in popular attitudes grants unlimited legitimate authority over the rest of the population. Little consideration is given to the liberal principle that the limits of government should be decided not by how a politician is appointed but in what fields he has power in the first place. The divine right of kings invoked by the seventeenth-century Stuart monarchs is echoed by today's democratic socialists.

Democracy and socialism in Scotland

The constitution of devolved Scotland was created as the apogee of democratic socialism, and it entrenches the power of the democratic state like nowhere else. The three dynamics are manifest very noticeably here. Indeed, arguably the Scottish Parliament is as a result the most powerful body of its kind in the world, within its jurisdiction.

The Scottish Parliament was established by politicians who believe wholeheartedly in the legitimacy of democracy. That, combined with the peculiar political circumstances of late twentieth-century Scotland and its relationship with the rest of the UK, means that there are almost no limits on its power save the constrictions of time, the bounds of its jurisdiction and four-yearly general elections.

The first two constrain the actions of all governments, and the latter all democracies. But other relics of the liberal past which constrain democracies in other countries, such as a revising chamber or the division of power between executive and legislature, are absent in Scotland. The Scottish Parliament does not even have to raise the money it spends from its own electorate!

The results are pernicious. Not only has the number of politicians rocketed in Scotland since devolution, but also the numbers of civil servants and the quantity of regulation passed as statutory instruments.

Public spending has soared so that it is now among the highest per capita in the Western world. Of the 62 bills passed by the parliament in its first term (1999–2003), only two can be said to be extending more freedom to the individual, and these are trivial.[3]

---

3   They concern the ability of St Andrews University to award certain
    medical degrees and where people can get married.

Graph 2: Statutory instruments applied in Scotland

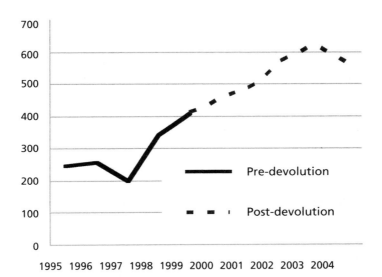

Source: HM Stationery Office

Of the others, many betray the insensitive presumptions about the legitimacy of democratic majorities discussed earlier. Bans on hunting, fur farming and now smoking in public places pay no heed to liberal scruple and the rights of the individual.

The smoking ban betrays a confusion at the heart of democratic government which is becoming pervasive. Since the government controls almost the entire health industry in Scotland, the performance of that sector is of central political importance. Since this is inevitably affected by the 'lifestyle' choices of Scots, the government is now intervening increasingly in individual tastes and choices. The fact that it has had to wrap up the ban in terms of employee (i.e. pub workers) health and safety adds lack of logic to the infringement of liberties. They might as well ban bus drivers from driving on the grounds that it is dangerous.

The problem with all this is that it makes the chances of liberal reform of the kind we discussed earlier in the chapter less likely to be implemented fully, and less likely to survive for long once matters improve. In short, the inbuilt tendency of the Scottish polity to spend taxpayers' money, to regulate and to legislate all mitigate against liberal reforms of the state sector designed to encourage individual decision making and responsibility.

Towards a liberal constitution in Scotland

The central philosophy which underpins the devolution settlement is that it reflects the settled will of the Scottish people. This implies that because a majority of Scots want something, responding to that desire is inherently legitimate. So the constitutional settlement assumes that an Executive based on a popular majority can and should apply itself to organizing society and attempting to solve the problems of the day.

As we have discussed, there are few limits on the Scottish Executive's actions apart from occasional general elections reaffirming its majority support, and time itself.

Constitutional debate revolves endlessly in a sterile argument about which voters should elect our politicians – UK voters, Scots voters, constituency-based ones, singly transferred voters, etc., instead of on the far more important matter of what politicians should be allowed to do.

However, the fact of devolution also presents an opportunity for Scotland. In questioning and then changing the way Scotland is governed, the process has shown an appetite for reform, and proved that change is possible. A slim chance therefore exists that we use this opportunity to re-examine our constitution and find a way of governing ourselves better than both the current arrangements and the previous ones.

This is not about nationalism, an essentially traditional philosophy concerned with the election of our rulers. For Scotland to be truly free the debate must shift to what powers politicians have at all. The method of selecting them, though important, is secondary.[4]

In a free Scotland, democratic mechanisms should be only some of many restrictions on the powers of politicians. Majoritarianism does not on its own protect our liberties, nor is it intrinsically legitimate. From the minority point of view, being ordered around by a majority is no better than being ordered around by a single dictator.

We have also seen how activist, interventionist, regulatory government leads to atrophied, over-regulated public services and industries, even when not directly state-owned.

So we must consider a set of rules, for both practical reasons, and ones of human rights, how to restrict their powers.

The traditional methods as espoused in the US and UK constitutions have proved helpful in slowing the accretion of powers by politicians, but ultimately have only delayed it.

While it is important to re-examine the division of power between executive and two chambers, as many have done in a Scottish context since devolution, that is not enough. These measures can improve the quality of legislation, and make it harder to achieve the necessary consensus to pass it in the first place. But once on the statute book it becomes very hard to repeal, and the overall *corpus juris* expands over time in any such democracy. We must therefore also

---

4 There is a very good case for electing politicians by lot, at least in the legislature. It delivers an accurate representation of popular opinion, but prevents political careerism.

look at three mechanisms which actually *limit* the accretion
of power by the state.

The first involves setting time limits on the longevity of
laws, perhaps dependent on the size of the majority by which
they were passed. There is no legitimate reason, democratic
or otherwise, why we should be bound by the rules of dead
politicians who we never even voted for. And there is no evidence that over time we have become better governed as the
statute book became fatter. Governments should therefore
have to spend part of their time assessing which of their predecessors' laws were worth keeping, and the overall size of
the statute book would be finite.

Secondly, taxation, the lifeblood of big government, should
require more universal consensus the higher it becomes. A
swingeing increase in taxes affecting many should need a
larger majority to pass.

Finally we must address the proper compartmentalizing of
different tiers of government. This is particularly important
in Scotland where nearly half of public expenditure is controlled by one elected body (the Scottish Parliament) that has
no responsibility for raising the revenue to pay for it. This
leads to a lack of proper accountability in political institutions. Instead there must be a clear coincidence of financial
and executive powers: each tier of government should raise
from its voters the money it is spending on their behalf.

The problem identified here is particularly acute in local
government, which currently raises only 20 per cent of the
money it spends. We have now reached an absurd point in
Scotland where the three levels of government interact in a
particularly obscure way which is hard to decipher for
trained economists, let alone the voting public. Essentially the
devolved Executive is adjusting the level of money it receives
from the UK government for central spending by loading
more central responsibilities onto local government without

passing on central funds. It has thus acquired a new, unintended and unaccounted-for tax-raising power, because local councils have to raise council tax to pay for the extra duties imposed upon them.

The dilemma with local government is that full fiscal powers at this level would either imply a quintupling of local taxes, or a removal of power to the centre which would make local authorities irrelevant to voters. Since they are widely ignored as it is, with turnout at local elections at an all time low, this risks leaving a largely unaccounted body of local politicians with little to do and low prospects – hardly a recipe for good governance.

I would propose a radical rethink of the structure and purpose of local government, therefore. Policy areas of national uniform importance, such as education and social work should be dealt with at a central level (preferably with measures designed to encourage individual responsibility and choice as we discussed above). Meanwhile issues which vary according to locality, such as planning, transport, street maintenance and rubbish collection should be devolved to much smaller local units based on natural geographic or community areas such as islands, dales or city neighbourhoods. They would be organized much more like companies, with greater 'shareholder' participation and the potential for dividend income as well as levies. Income could be generated from road tolls and the granting of development rights. The incentives would work in favour of good services but low rates, and environmentally sensitive development to maximize revenues without damaging property prices.

*   *   *

Tom Miers is Executive Director of the Policy Institute, an Edinburgh-based think-tank established to promote liberal market values and solutions. Prior to joining the Policy Institute he worked for the Institute of Economic Affairs in London. He lives in Edinburgh.

BRIAN MONTEITH

8

A view from inside:
the failure of devolution

IT IS BEYOND ARGUMENT that devolution has come as a great disappointment to the Scottish public. Much was said in the 18 years of Conservative government about how life could be so much better if only we had our own Scottish Parliament. Even more audacious claims about its low running costs and ability to revive Scotland's economy, culture and environment were made in the run up to the referendum of September 1997.

But the disenchantment of the electorate after only the Parliament's first four-year term was recorded for all to see in the 2003 Scottish Parliament elections. Less than half of those entitled to vote – a humiliating 49 per cent – turned out, despite regular cajoling by the First Minister and politicians of all parties.

Since then the most recent surveys suggest that the levels of dissatisfaction have grown. It is not hard to see why. Consider the following sample from a wealth of disappointing facts that compare recent figures with those of 1999.

In health, waiting lists have lengthened from 90,062 to 112,052 while the median outpatient and inpatient waits have grown. Outpatients waiting over a year have increased by 868 to 7,609. Meanwhile, more non-clinical staff have been recruited than doctors and nurses combined.

Crimes and offences have reached the highest level on record, coming in at 1,071,077 – up from 940,153. While some crimes have fallen, fire-raising and vandalism, rape and attempted rape and handling an offensive weapon have all increased since 1999.

Drug crime makes especially bad reading. This has risen from 31,870 to 40,465 while the number of Methadone prescriptions rose from 214,677 to 387,965 and annual drug-related deaths climbed to 317 in the same period.

In education, incidents of classroom violence have increased from 1,898 to 6,899 while the number of schools that cater for children with special educational needs has fallen by 15. Particularly notable was the handling of the SQA crisis of 2000. Whilst the beginnings of the new Higher Still system predated devolution, and indeed the Labour victory of 1997, it should be remembered that Labour had been in power for more than three years and the then Education Minister, Sam Galbraith, for more than a year when it broke. The inability of the Parliament to have the Minister take responsibility for his poor handling of the crisis left many dissatisfied with the level of accountability.

In higher education the Scottish Parliament 'abolished' tuition fees – or did it? A cursory examination of Scottish university websites establishes the truth that the fees actually still exist but are paid on behalf of the student by the Scottish Executive through the Student Awards Agency for Scotland. Scottish students were always funded in the past through the Scottish Education Department and the current arrangement could have been handled by the old Scottish Office if it had wanted to. What the Scottish Parliament did do was introduce a graduate endowment tax that takes money from old students to give to new students.

In the economy, such has been the growth of public spending that the state's share of economic activity has grown from

47 per cent to nearly 54 per cent. The private sector is being
crowded out with the business start-up rate per 10,000
marooned at 29 while it has climbed to over 40 in England.

The number of *manufacturing jobs*, which had increased in
the 1990s, has fallen from 336,000 to 284,000, while the
numbers employed in fishing and farming have also dropped
significantly. The Scottish business rate started at par with the
English poundage but was quickly raised to nine per cent
higher. Only after a persistent campaign is it now planned to
bring it back to par by 2007.

Personal taxes have fared no better. In the six years since
1999 the average Band D Council Tax has risen by almost a
third from £849 to £1,094.

Homelessness was an emotionally charged issue in the
1990s so it would come as a shock for the public to find that
the number of people in temporary accommodation nearly
doubled from 3,864 to 7,135, while the number of people
living in bed and breakfasts practically trebled, from 413 to
1,206.

The cost of government has grown dramatically. Advertis-
ing has risen from £3 million to £9.5 million, civil servant
numbers have increased, government special advisers have
increased and the executive spin-doctors have gone from 41
to 91.

The outrageous *construction cost of the parliament building* is well recorded. But the design's complexity, idiosyncrasy
and self-indulgence has delivered an embarrassingly high
annual maintenance cost of £1.3 million. The overall running
cost of having a Parliament should cause the most worry, now
coming in at £63 million – that's four secondary schools or
one hospital every year.

Policy failure not institutional failure

These statistics, had they unfolded under a Conservative government in London with its Scottish Secretary of State in Edinburgh, would have seen protests from the very Labour and Liberal Democrat politicians whose performance has been so lamentable. But this is not a failure in the institution itself. The blame must fairly and squarely be placed upon the policies of the Scottish Executive coalition parties.

In England various public services are showing some signs of improvement. This is due to the modernization and accompanying productivity gains that have been rejected by the Scottish Executive.

We have a devolution settlement that owes much to the reaction of formerly devout unionist Labour MPs to four Tory election victories. They threw in their lot in with a Scottish Parliament that might halt Thatcherism at Hadrian's Wall and give socialism a last hurrah in Scotland. The irony is that we have ended up with New Labour stopping at Hexham and Old Labour continuing to fossilize in Scotland.

Thus, to blame the Parliament for this is going too far. The *policy direction* is the choice of the Scottish people. But it is a choice that could in future change.

It is, however, important to remember that the SNP, as the main opposition party, is also signed up to the social democrat model that advocates more spend and waste policies.

The Liberal Democrat group of MSPs has also regularly shown itself to be on the Left of the Labour MSPs by pushing for ever greater and greater expansion of the welfare state. If there's a policy that advocates making some public service 'free', then you can bet your house that it was thought up by either Tommy Sheridan's Scottish Socialist Party or the Scottish Liberal Democrats. 'Free' personal care, 'free' bus trips, 'free' school meals, 'free' eye and dental checks, 'free' swimming lessons, 'free' prescriptions: both parties push some or all of these policies and are resisted, often unsuccessfully, by Scottish Labour.

The blame for the failure of devolution to improve the standard and quality of public services and meet public expectations must, therefore, be laid at the ruling political consensus rather than the institution.

Success? What success?

That is not to say that devolution has not had its successes. One must, however, discount those that can be put down to political action that would have been possible by the old Scottish Office, just as I have discounted why so many of the failures are due to the faulty policies – rather than a faulty institution. The creation of a National Theatre of Scotland illustrates this point.

Anyone who participated in the debate surrounding the case for a Scottish Parliament will recall how so many of Scotland's cultural participants in the performing arts thought Scotland would blossom once it had its own parliament. Not only would the MSPs be able to vote through more money and support new initiatives, but also the mere creation of the Parliament would create a new mood about the land, a new enthusiasm and inspiration for cultural work to excel. Culture would be given a new priority.

And yet since 1999 there has probably been no group of people that has voiced greater disappointment than those who insisted Scotland's cultural renaissance would come under devolution.

Scotland's ability to support cultural institutions of international reputation has been seriously damaged. The trauma suffered by Scottish Opera is the most dramatic example.

Meanwhile funding at the Scottish Arts Council has in some years only kept pace with inflation while in the year Lord Watson was one of the five culture Ministers since 1999, he actually saw his department budget fall in real terms. The farce of the Cultural Commission, with a report running to hundreds of pages of bureaucratic jargon, more than a hundred unprioritized recommendations and a subsequent question-begging reorganization by the arts minister typify the confusion of the response.

Compare this to the fact that it was a Scotland without a parliament in the 1960s that saw the creation of Scottish Opera, Scottish Ballet, the Royal Lyceum Theatre Company and the Citizens and Traverse Theatres and one can see that devolution is not crucial to cultural renaissance. Indeed the most significant change to artistic activity in Scotland over the last 20 years has come from London through the introduction of the National Lottery. It was the Conservative Scottish Office that had, in the 1990s, established a Scottish Arts Council separate from the parent UK body and created Scottish Screen.

Yes, the Parliament's Education, Culture and Sport Committee, upon which I served for its first four years, was able to breathe new life into the concept of a national theatre that had been waiting in the wings for some time.

It is reasonable to believe, however, that had a Tory Scottish Office been presented with the commissioning model for a national theatre that was proposed to the committee by Kenny Ireland in 2000, it would have been only too pleased to adopt the idea to show how it was acting in Scotland's cultural interests. The party of the late Nicky Fairbairn and George Younger has, after all, impeccable credentials in supporting Scotland's theatre.

To sum up, the creation of the National Theatre of Scotland cannot be claimed as the direct result of devolution for it was just as likely to happen without it. This example is true of many of the claims made on behalf of devolution.

More is less

Another claim often made is that devolution has allowed more than 90 acts of the Scottish Parliament to be passed, the majority of which would simply not have found the time of day at Westminster. In strict terms of parliamentary time this claim cannot be refuted. But it measures the quantity of the cloth rather than the quality – which is less than what one should expect.

Nor does it take account of the need for any government operating with only one parliament at its disposal to prioritize its legislative proposals, and in so doing make sure that they are of enough importance to merit consideration.

For instance the process of land reform was initiated by the Law Commission pre-devolution while the Conservatives were in power. That the Land Reform Act went much further under the executive coalition than a Conservative government would have sought to go I do not dispute, but I do dispute the suggestion that Tories would on no account have seen some advantage in introducing such laws in response to the Law Commission's report.

Other legislation such as the abolition of Section 2a, commonly known as Section 28 in England, would simply have been processed with the same proposals for England. This would have meant the wish of the overwhelming majority of the Scots public that the repeal be rejected would have been acted upon by the House of Lords in a way that two Scottish parliamentary committees that handled the bill in their scrutinizing role failed to do.

It's not as if Scottish legislation did not happen in Westminster. It did when it was recognized that it deserved priority, such as the Education Act 1980 and the Education Acts of 1987 and 1988. Indeed I would suggest that were there to be less legislation coming forward at Holyrood then greater time could be spent scrutinizing the drafting quality as well as debating the likely effects and impacts of these bills.

For instance the Education Act of 2000 has not just once but twice required further parliamentary time to correct faulty drafting that had not been picked up at any stage.

Ludwig Mies van der Rohe famously said 'less is more' when describing his approach to modern architecture. When considering the approach of the Scottish Parliament to legislation one could fairly say 'more is less'.

Scrutiny? What scrutiny?

This brings me on to another claim that requires to be examined: that devolution has brought more scrutiny and accountability. One has to be careful to ask the questions, scrutiny of what and accountability of whom?

There has certainly been more scrutiny of all sorts of organizations – from the Scottish Executive (in a manner that the Scottish Office was very rarely scrutinized) to public bodies such as Scottish Water and even essentially private organizations such as the Scottish Football Association (in its involvement of public projects such as Hampden as well as its governance of football).

I welcome this development when it leads to greater public accountability, but that's what it has to be about; accountability. Scrutiny without accountability is merely political voyeurism.

So when I talk of greater scrutiny I mean the scrutiny of legislation – and here I feel that the Scottish Parliament's record is not so impressive. Indeed I would say that at best the jury is not so much out as booked in to a hotel for the foreseeable future.

I genuinely fear the unicameral process that Scotland's devolution employs, as I do not believe that it scrutinizes Bills in enough detail thus allowing poor law to be passed. Nor is it subject to the democratic checks that are necessary to protect minority interests or from bad laws being rushed through by democratic mob rule in the heat of a public outcry.

The stage one inquiry considers the principles of Bills and publishes a report. On the rare occasion when committees have recommended changes to a Bill at second stage there is certainly no guarantee that this will happen. This was shown when the committee report on Lord Watson's 2001 Protection of Wild Mammals (Scotland) Bill, which was a member's Bill and should therefore have been easier to change, was completely ignored and the Bill proceeded unscathed.

In my experience it is only at the second stage that details are properly analysed and tested, but by then committee members are most definitely being whipped so that there is little likelihood of amendment unless the Executive gives its consent. By the third stage, when all members of parliament have a vote, but when the whipping is correspondingly more necessary for party discipline, the chances of amendment are even slimmer.

Unlike the bicameral process at Westminster there is no check or balance that can delay a Bill for a year for further consideration – or have it amended by politicians who, with a different mandate, can take a different view. Add to this the quite legitimate claim already voiced by a number of my MSP colleagues from other parties that the second- and third-stage processes are so rushed that members are often left with two-minute speeches to debate the merits of legislation that can determine the livelihoods of people or their businesses.

The debacle at the third stage of the Executive's licensing legislation was a typical example of the lack of time made available for proper consideration. The plain fact is that the current system provides insufficient scrutiny of a high enough calibre or a court of appeal where people can be given time to reconsider the merits of certain clauses.

The Standards in Scottish Schools Act 2000 is another example of legislation that could and should have been better scrutinized. Assurances were accepted on funding that should have been tested more strongly. The Auditor General has himself drawn attention to the difficulties of the Executive's amendments to special educational needs that were not financially quantified. My experience with other Bills, such as the Bill to ban smoking in all public spaces, has not been any better. The pressure to race through the discussion of amendments so that some arguments are not heard is especially apparent.

As for accountability, I believe the claim that ministers are more accountable remains not proven. Sam Galbraith's handling of the SQA fiasco would have been better tested in Westminster. Censure and even resignation would certainly have stood a better chance.

In my experience of the SQA inquiry held by the Education, Culture and Sport Committee – generally held up as one of the best such inquiries – the members were able to agree to criticisms of the SQA officials, Her Majesty's Inspectorate of Education and Education Department officials, but of Ministers? Of course not. Labour and Liberal Democrat members simply refused to countenance any criticism, not even a censure of Galbraith for going away on holiday when he knew that the system was about to fail. Accountability exists for some but not others.

For achievements in policy development that have brought about improvements in public services or have created valuable new institutions or better ways of doing things in Scotland to be credited to devolution it must be demonstrated that it would have been impossible for the old Scottish Office to have taken the same action were Labour or a Labour coalition to have been in power. Examples of these are few.

The most significant achievement must be the creation by Act of Parliament in 2000 of Audit Scotland and the Auditor General for Scotland through the Public Finance and Accountability (Scotland) Act. Until I joined the Parliament's Audit Committee as its convener in 2003 I have to say that its work, and that of the Auditor General, had not registered on my radar to any great extent. My appreciation of the change to the auditing of Scottish public bodies and the efforts made to find value for money and establish best practice grew very quickly once I became immersed in the process myself.

It should be remembered that prior to this act the auditing of public bodies was handled in Scotland by the National Audit Office and reported to Westminster by the Comptroller General. Any parliamentary scrutiny happened at Westminster through the Public Accounts Committee, which met twice weekly every week of a sitting – even with such a busy schedule such was its workload that Scottish bodies, never mind Scottish area bodies (such as local health boards) were given practically no public scrutiny.

Now the Audit Committee considers reports produced by the Auditor General where the facts are agreed between Audit Scotland and the audited body before publication. This process is vital as it means MSPs focus around what caused these facts rather than be distracted in a pointless dispute about their accuracy. As a result of this system the Audit Committee has in the last five years followed up on a number of the Auditor General's reports that have resulted in real change to procedure or policy saving millions, improving outcomes or both.

Here to stay

No matter the number of policy failures, or overstated claims that are made for devolution, I do not believe that having been created the Scottish Parliament should now be abolished. It is, I believe, here to stay and will not be going away.

Poll after poll, survey after survey shows that rather than abolish the Parliament, the Scottish public would rather it had more powers. Research also shows a growth in people feeling more Scottish than British so that this group is now the dominant one. Thirty years ago the Scots felt British and Scottish.

However, I still believe that the Scottish Parliament remains a threat to the union between Scotland and England. It has yet to be tested when there are governments of different parties in London and Edinburgh – and in practical terms too many of the performance figures are poorer than what was being achieved in 1999, and often even worse than 1997! The public reaction to these situations could still rip the union asunder.

There are, however, times in politics when you have to recognize that the Rubicon has been crossed and there is no going back. For the only Right-of-centre party in Scotland to advocate the abolition of the Holyrood parliament would simply define it as anti-Scottish and send it into electoral oblivion – further weakening the whole union.

Although the current devolution settlement was shaped by the constitutional convention and supported in the referendum by the SNP, Liberal Democrat and Labour parties it is chiefly Labour's devolution settlement. It was Labour's Scotland Act, nobody else's. While it was designed to deliver devolution it also had to ensure that the socialist citadel of Scotland would not succumb to an assault from nationalism or liberation by free-market ideas. It has been designed to preserve in a consensual aspic Labour's domination of Scotland at every level, allowing change only at the margins. So far it has succeeded; even the introduction of the single transferable vote system will not lead to significant change in who rules Labour's municipal fiefdoms. It is also designed to work with a Labour government in Westminster; the model does not reveal how it would survive the obvious conflicts that will come from differing economic approaches being taken in London and Edinburgh – or other policy clashes.

A Conservative victory in the UK, or rather Holyrood's reaction to one, remains the greatest threat to the union, for it could provoke displays of nationalism in the Labour and Liberal Democrat parties that will simply fuel the fire of the independence movement. Ironically it will also leave the Scottish Tory party beached on a sandbank of indecision – should it set off attempting to defend a Westminster government that will be constantly portrayed as being a threat to Scotland's interests and thus risk electoral oblivion yet again, or should it attack the party of government that it works to elect by rejecting some of the core beliefs that it is supposed to stand for? No one in the Scottish Tories has asked this question, let alone offered an answer.

It is therefore important that if the union is to be preserved that other parties that tried but failed to amend the Scotland Act consider what improvements might still be made that will make it far more politically sustainable when it faces the various constitutional shocks and tests that it has still to endure.

A block grant funding system that does not make politicians accountable for what they spend because they do not have to raise it skews the system in favour of throwing money at every problem, and works against establishing clear priorities from scarcer resources and extracting value for money. The block grant is an institutional impediment to good government and contributes to the poor performance that devolution is currently saddled with.

If devolution is to have a real chance of working rather than delivering independence by default, it must have a more accountable system of finance, offer more effective scrutiny of legislation and provide greater accountability of the Scottish public sector.

If the structure of devolution is built on these more solid foundations I believe it stands a far better chance of delivering more demonstrable achievements, that will not only be worthwhile in themselves but can also usher in a more open reassessment of the policies that are currently failing.

So what can be done? Here are three approaches that could be adopted.

Financial accountability

The difficulties of the Parliament's public service delivery are directly related to the detachment that the Scottish Executive has, and indeed most MSPs have, from economic reality. The block grant system (and the accompanying Barnett Formula that determines what increases, or theoretically what reductions, are made) has created a dependency culture that is damaging to Scotland and the union. It is my belief that it is no longer justifiable or sustainable – economically or politically.

If localism is good – and I say it is, because it means councils being responsive and accountable to local taxpayers – then it must also mean the Scottish Parliament, the Welsh and Northern Ireland assemblies, also being accountable to their national taxpayers.

This means that the current level of structural economic subsidies must over, say, the length of two parliaments, be phased out and the local institutions raise, either directly or through the assignation of taxes gathered in their fiefdoms, far more – or even all – of the money that they spend. This would mean Holyrood would cut or raise taxes, and borrow money, within set limits. Politicians who feel the pain of taxpayers think twice before making more demands on the public purse; they learn to prioritize and become self-disciplined.

The idea that the number of taxpayers in Scotland is greatly lower than the rest of the UK is a myth. It is only slightly below the UK average. What is different is the number of public-sector employees due to the dominance of the state in the economy. Creating a Scottish Treasury that will put its own internal disciplines on departmental spending and can point to the costs of policies when others only want to consider the benefits is a prerequisite for a prudent public sector that allows enough room for the private sector to create the wealth that it lives off.

Every day that this policy is resisted makes Scotland more dependent upon – and thus at greater risk from – separation from England.

A second chamber

The unfinished business that is Tony Blair's assault on the composition of the UK's Upper House must be addressed by a future Westminster government. The value of the Lords is regularly demonstrated when, even now, after the changes that Blair has made, it makes amendments or rejects proposals that have met with meeker opposition in the Lower House. Whatever reform of the composition of the Upper House's membership brings we can expect it to continue to have powers to amend and delay legislation from the Lower House.

A newly reformed Upper House should aim to establish a credibility with the British electorate that it has not previously enjoyed. This credibility can only come from the majority of its members being elected.

While I personally prefer a high proportion of elected members, I see no reason to become too excited if that percentage is 60 per cent or 80 per cent. To ensure that the Upper House enjoys a degree of thinking independent from any ruling government its members should be elected on a long once-only term of office that lasts beyond the potential full term of the Lower House's Executive, say, for seven or even 11 years.

By all means let there be some ex-officio members, such as members of the justiciary, and allow a small number of appointed members, because limited party patronage has a role to play in providing quick routes for talented people that have for good reason stayed out of party politics, but the proportions between these groups are not crucial so long as the credibility that an electoral mandate brings is established in the public's mind.

While that reform is being secured, the role of those that represent Scotland in it should then be considered. As a Scot I would urge that we have the Scottish members of the Upper House, called Peers, Senators, or what you will, regularly sitting in Scotland as a revising chamber, considering legislation from the Scottish Parliament. They would have a Scottish mandate but could bring different strengths and more independent thought to our legislative process.

Given that legislation in England on, say, education goes before the new Upper House then why should inadequately scrutinized Scottish bills on education not do the same? Why could the Scottish legislation not go before *only* its Scottish members with them sitting in Scotland, probably at Holyrood?

This arrangement has the attraction of keeping costs to the minimum in that the new representatives would *already* have been created with their own existing budget with no additional buildings required. Their powers could be similar to those already held for UK or English Bills, in that amendments could be made and Bills delayed subject to a time bar.

Such an arrangement would, I believe, increase the quality of the scrutiny, provide a potential brake on unpopular legislation that had not been in a party's manifesto (the abolition of Section 2a in 2000, the banning of smoking in 2005, etc.) and give a check to an unbridled tyranny of the majority.

Scrutiny? Yes, please

Taking the example of the Parliament's Audit Committee and the way that the Auditor General lays reports before Parliament that the Audit Committee can consider, and if so minded institute its own enquiry, we should consider what similar lessons there could be for other committees to make various public bodies more accountable.

For instance, would it not be possible for the Parliament's committee with responsibility for arts to consider annually the work of the national cultural institutions such as the galleries, libraries, museums, Scottish Opera, Scottish Ballet and National Theatre as well as the many orchestras and festivals, not to mention the various quangos that relate to them, namely the Scottish Arts Council, Scottish Screen, Historic Scotland and others? As the list is long, to avoid repetition and allow for in-depth scrutiny there would be some rotation, such as at least every four years.

Under current arrangements such bodies are monitored by the Scottish Executive's education department – but neither the quangos nor the department are put under regular and serious scrutiny on the policy or the outputs of the quangos and the institutions. Now that we have a gaggle of MSPs and all the parliamentary facilities, do we really need a quango to provide arm's length objectivity, and if we decide we do, do we really need a department with so many staff to monitor it as well? Can the MSPs not take on a greater load depending what quangos their committee might cover?

Of course many MSPs might say they are very busy on committees already. But Andrew Arbuckle MSP was not entirely wrong when he laid the charge that MSPs find work to do. It's called Parkinson's Law and the real question therefore is can they use their time to greater effect by scrutinizing the work of public bodies and holding them or their political bosses to account?

Scottish Water is an example. A public body that spends hundreds of thousands attracting top executives with salaries that match what they might earn in the private sector, it operates under a regulatory body and departmental officials that are paid a fifth of the management's salaries (so how do they know better?). Who really knows best, the management, the regulators, the department officials and the minister? Are they all needed? Is the cost of all these tiers of government necessary? Could a parliamentary committee not take on the role of some of the officials?

Then there are the various Czars for health, crime, food, drugs and alcohol and all sorts of initiatives. Who are they accountable to? Were there to be a more formal relationship between quangos and committees, were some agencies such as Her Majesty's Inspectorate of Education to report directly to Parliament rather than the Executive – such as the Auditor General does – then the committees could be given the role of scrutinizing these blossoming public bodies.

Rather than initiating enquiries so that they look busy when there is a real job of scrutiny and accountability to be done, committees would at last become the focus of attention at Holyrood for they would be doing something far more worthwhile than publishing reports that are ignored. The effect would be to win over the public by showing that its committee work is indeed effective and not just the self-indulgent hyperbole of devolution devotees.

There is hope

Devolution will always turn out to be more expensive to deliver than the Houses of Parliament at Westminster. And many of the policy outcomes would have been possible by the Scottish Office by simply changing political control. There is, however, no going back to the past system. Despite the public's disenchantment with devolution, I do still believe that it can be made to work far better than it is and so avoid independence becoming inevitable.

It requires the advocates of devolution to recognize that the current model is not the finished article and requires reform. There are many approaches that can be taken. Here I have concentrated on the case for better scrutiny of legislation through a revising chamber that already will have its costs met and need not be elitist or anti-democratic. I have argued the need to address the corrupting influence of our dependency on the block grant. And finally I put the case for giving MSPs a more defined role in holding public bodies to account. It should be possible to better establish their work ethic, while reducing costs and improving policy outcomes.

There is hope. But it requires the Scottish Parliament to come out of denial, confront its demons and offer real solutions.

*   *   *

Brian Monteith is a List MSP for Central Scotland and Fife. He served as Conservative spokesman on finance, local government and public services, and as spokesman on education, the arts, culture and sport. He was national coordinator of the No, No campaign in the Scottish devolution referendum. He resigned the Conservative whip to become an independent in late 2005 after the departure of Conservative leader David McLetchie.

Society and Welfare

FRASER NELSON

9
A tale of three Scotlands

SCOTLAND IS A NATION of contradictions. We are a rich country. But we have third-world levels of deprivation. We spend more of our national wealth on health than almost any country in the world. Yet our life expectancy remains the worst in Western Europe.

We are a nation famed for its genius and invention. Yet our business start-up rate is the lowest in the country.[1] We invented the free-market economics which made America a superpower. Yet we ourselves imported a model of the Scandinavian-style big state.

A nation that has punched above its weight for generations now finds itself on the ropes of the world economy. It is coached by a political class that sees its job as managing decline. To get back in the fight, we need radical new thinking on the role of government.

---

1   There was a 5.4 per cent increase in VAT registrations in Scotland between 1994 and 2004, less than half the 12.8 per cent rise seen across the UK. Figures from the Bank of Scotland, *Scottish Economic Trends*, November 2005.

Not one, but three Scotlands

On paper, Scotland can look a terrifying place to live. Glasgow, its largest city, is the murder capital of Europe[2] – surpassing even Belfast. Its depopulation is fastest amongst the under-40s, leading to 10,500 places permanently falling off the school roll each year.[3]

Applications for official homeless status easily outnumber applications for university places.[4] Indeed, one in every 100 Scots applied to be considered homeless in 2004–05, a caseload which has more than trebled since 1980.

Yet this portrait of an ageing, depopulating, pauperized and even murderous nation will seem utterly incongruous not just to visitors, but to middle Scotland. They see a healthy, confident small nation that offers quality of life that Londoners can only dream of.

When Islington decamps to Edinburgh for the Festival, it looks around with envy. House prices are still two-thirds of England's and less than half of London's[5] but salaries are broadly comparable[6] – as are the restaurants. Not to mention the scenery within an hour's drive.

---

2   Scottish Executive, *Homicides in Scotland 2003* (November 2004). Table 18 gives murder rates per million citizens. Glasgow was top with 58.7, Belfast second, 55.9. Then came Amsterdam (31.1), Brussels (28.7) and Vienna (28.4).

3   Scottish Executive, *Teacher Workforce Planning for 2004/05*. Contains projections until 2013.

4   In 2004–05, Scottish councils received 57,020 applications for homeless status, up from 15,466 in 1980. The full study is in a statistical bulletin Operation of the Homeless Persons legislation in Scotland: national and local authority analyses 2004–05.

5   Average house cost, £119,000 in Scotland at end-2004, £180,248 in England, and £273,000 in London according to the Office of the Deputy Prime Minister. Data available online at www.odpm.gov.uk/embedded_object.asp?id=1156112.

6   Salary data, Labour market statistics 2005, ONS.

If you are middle class, the odds are you live in one of the neighbourhoods of Prime Scotland: one of the world's most desirable spots. The statistics about poverty, heart disease, crime, economic sluggishness and vagrancy do not apply to you, or to those around you.

But there is another world, where the opposite is true. It exists in the sink housing estates, what we can call Third Scotland. It lives in social segregation. If you are poor, Scotland is one of the worst places in Europe in which to be.

In between the two, we have Second Scotland – the lower half of those who work, and earn. For here, life is neither particularly good nor particularly bad – but getting better. Rather than look at problem cities (Glasgow and Dundee are frequently named UK black spots) the research allows us to zero in on the pockets of poverty that make up Third Scotland – whether they are rural enclaves or dilapidated corners of cities.

Third Scotland exists in a strange jobless oasis, little welfare ghettos inside a country where the economy is strong and demand for labour is high. It exists because of redistribution of wealth: a well-meaning project of redistribution, flawed by its shallow materialism.

Most worryingly, life for the poorest in Britain is getting worse. A UK government survey[7] shows the incomes of the poorest 10 per cent in Britain are getting lower, while things they must buy are getting more expensive.

Prime Scotland and Third Scotland are not far apart geographically. But for all their juxtaposition, they seldom meet. The cities are designed so the Scottish underclass is

---

7   DWP, *Households Below Average Income 2003–04*. Supplementary Table A2 shows weekly income of the poorest 10 per cent falling from £91 in 2001–02, £90 in 2002–03 and £88 in 2003–04. Data can be downloaded at www.dwp.gov.uk/asd/hbai/hbai2004/excel_files/supplementary_tables/suptabs_a_excel_hbai05.xls#'a2'!A1.

concentrated in the council estates, where it is largely ignored by police.

This is an economic as well as a human disaster. Scotland can never fire on all cylinders while a sixth of her population is dependent on welfare. Yet the benefit system gives a clear and rational reason to prefer welfare to work.

No consideration of Scotland's future is complete without a consideration of its underclass – a word Scottish Labour does not like to use, knowing it is a phenomenon that has grown for decades under the negligent eye of its local authorities.

Scotland's underclass

A boy born today in Glasgow can expect to die earlier than a child born in China.[8] It says much for the problems of Glasgow's deprived East End that this statistic is for the city as a whole – including some of the most desirable suburbs in Britain.

Male life expectancy in Castlemilk (65 years) is closer to Baghdad (61 years) than Bearsden (78 years). A boy born in Castlemilk is four times as likely to live in a single-parent household, and there is a 55 per cent chance his mother smoked during her pregnancy.

Yet even this is not Scotland's rock bottom. A boy born in Calton, central Glasgow, has a life expectancy of 53.9 years – closer to Cameroon (51 years) than Castlemilk. Occasionally,

---

8   Male life expectancy in Glasgow was 69.3 over 2002 to 2004. The World Bank figure for China during that period was 70. Scottish data from General Register Office, 6 October 2005, 'Life expectancy for administrative areas within Scotland, 2002–2004'.

the city boasts[9] of being the 'youngest in Scotland'. Early death of its elderly is partly why.

At the end of the Second World War, male UK life expectancy was 63 years – two decades more than at the First World War. Yet this is a level of progress that at least a dozen areas of Glasgow and one part of Edinburgh (Granton) has yet to reach.

But a Scottish problem? Absolutely not. A child born in Nether Williamston,[10] in West Lothian, can expect to live until 87 – higher than any country in the world, towering above Sweden which holds the number one slot with its life expectancy of 80.4 years.

In fact, if you look at Middle Scotland you will find areas where the top AB social classes own at least a quarter of the houses and the life expectancy is a handsome 77.3 years. Look at areas where the welfare dependent make up at least a quarter of houses, and it drops to 64 years.

Glasgow, as a city, has long been caricatured as a den of drunkenness and ill-health. This is unfair. Its problem is social inequality, not disease. Citizens of Milngavie, Lenzie and Clarkston (all in Prime Scotland) can live until their 80s. But men in Drumchapel, Ibrox, Easterhouse, Parkhead and Dalmarnock are unlikely to make it to the pensionable age of 65 years.

So this is not a nationwide problem, or even a west of Scotland problem. It is a function of poverty in Scotland, which is concentrated in ghettos where welfare dependency is the highest, not necessarily where wages are lowest.

---

9   'Glasgow Set to be Youngest City' by Jonathan Paisley, *Evening Times*. Available on www.eveningtimes.co.uk/hi/news/5028443.html.
10 The full social data for Nether Williamston and the EH54 postcode is found in a PDF file on www.phis.org.uk/upload/pdf2/WestLothian/LivingstonBrucefield.pdf.

For example, the 2001 census found an average household income of £22,000 in Dunkeld, Perthshire and £24,000 in Fullarton, Irvine – but their life expectancy was 79 years and 64 years respectively. But Fullarton's welfare dependency was three times higher.

Scotland's welfare trap

Incapacity benefit is the prison warden of Scotland's underclass. In theory, it is a payment for those – of any social class – who are physically or mentally unable to work. In practice, it is open to wide abuse and can be converted into never-ending unemployment benefit.

Without it, there would be far fewer welfare ghettos because the able-bodied would be obliged to find work – which is in plentiful supply in a low-unemployment country[11] like Scotland. Instead, children grow up aspiring to sign on to incapacity benefit.

This is entirely rational. When welfare competes with low pay, people will logically choose benefits – for the same reason that workers in Prime Scotland will take an early retirement package if they can make the sums stack up. It's a no-brainer.

Today, UK ministers believe[12] that only a third of the 2.7 million claiming the benefit in February 2005 were genuinely unable to work. Britain's immigration surge[13] is driven by the

---

11 Scottish unemployment was 5.4 per cent in November 2004 according to the ONS, almost half the Euro zone's 10.5 per cent.
12 'Most incapacity benefit claimants could work, says minister', Patrick Wintour, the *Guardian*, 15 December 2004.
13 In 2004, immigration to the UK reached a record 582,000. Full data online from the ONS: www.statistics.gov.uk/CCI/nugget.asp?ID=260& Pos=1&ColRank=1&Rank=176.

large economic appetite for unskilled labour which the natives will no longer do.

Taken together with housing support, disability living allowance and other parts of the welfare system, it can pay more than the minimum wage. This is not a matter of sloth or sponging: for those on the breadline, it is the rational choice.

But it has now so defaced Scotland's workforce that in February 2005 there were 281,500 claiming it.[14] As always, this nationwide figure hides the black spots exposed by the 2001 Census: 49 per cent in Dalmarnock, Glasgow, 44 per cent in Calton, 31 per cent in Craigmillar, Edinburgh.

If Scotland's incapacity benefit population would live together, they would outnumber the combined populations of Dunfermline, Falkirk, Kilmarnock, Paisley, Perth and Stirling.

Family break-up soon follows incapacity benefit. Robbed of its economic function, the family is often the first casualty of welfare dependency: data shows a direct link between the two. The most deprived areas are denoted by high single-parent figures.

This affects vast swathes of Scotland. In Dalmarnock, 41 per cent of households are occupied by a single parent: in Calton, 30 per cent and in Drumchapel, 27 per cent. In Prime Scotland, the figure is far lower: 7 per cent in Milngavie, 6.4 per cent in Clarkston and 5.6 per cent in Nether Williamston. This matters because successive studies[15] have shown that, for those on the breadline, children in a stable family are far more likely to finish school, find a job and avoid drugs and

14 Department for Work and Pensions, Incapacity Benefit and Severe Disablement Allowance Quarterly Summary Statistics: February 2005, Table IB2.3.

15 The Heritage Foundation, based in Washington DC, collated US and UK studies. They are available free online at www.heritage.org/research/family/index.cfm.

crime. Simply put, the odds facing a lone parent are far more daunting than those for a strong family.

This was the guiding principle behind the successful American welfare reform in 1995. Yet the family is utterly missing from UK welfare policy. The current political orthodoxy fails to acknowledge the crucial role that it plays. Indeed, the Centre for Policy Studies has found[16] that the current tax and benefits system is so perverse that an average family would receive £5,000 more in benefits than it paid in tax if it split up – and would pay £7,000 more in tax if it stayed together.

These are the dynamics across the UK. But they hit Scotland the hardest because incapacity benefit took root after the deindustrialization of the 1980s when the then Conservative government encouraged people from unemployment to incapacity benefit.

This is because, since the 1920s, the life of Scotland's manufacturing sector was artificially prolonged[17] by central planners in London who thought that the best way to combat unemployment was to commission some more metal-bashing.

It was a double whammy: Scotland's economy was kept bogged down too long in manufacturing, and when this died the workforce was pushed onto incapacity benefit. It was a form of economically decommissioning humanity: and a scandalous waste of life. Unemployment – technically defined – has been effectively slain in today's Scotland. But this is a shallow victory when joblessness remains endemic.

This is why building contractors on the council house refurbishment project under way in Glasgow over the

---

16 'The Price of Parenthood' by Jill Kirby for the Centre for Policy Studies 2005 can be downloaded as a PDF attachment on www.cps.org.uk/pdf/pub/396.pdf.
17 Correspondence from successive Scotland Secretaries showing the planning of various manufacturing schemes, starting with Sir James Gilmour in 1924, is produced in *The Scottish Office 1919–59* (Scottish Historical Society, 1992).

summer of 2005 had to bus in workers from outside the city.[18] Businesses looking for white-collar workers find the labour pool sucked dry by government.

Scotland's businesses are facing a pincer movement: lack of unskilled labour on one hand, and fierce competition for new graduates by an ever-expanding bureaucracy which pays top dollar and offers good pensions and easier hours.

It has never made less sense to work for the UK private sector. People in government are paid more,[19] retire earlier and can look forward to a more generous pensions package. Scotland's wealth-creating private sector exists in the endeavours of 1.7 million people.[20]

Scotland's share of the UK economy (%)

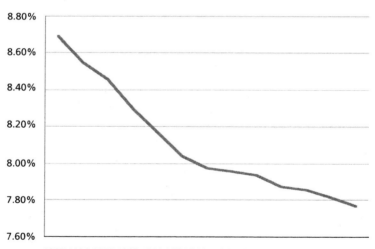

18 Evidence collected by a Scottish MP on condition of anonymity.
19 Annual Survey of Hours and Earnings 2005 shows median public sector pay is £375 a week, and median private sector pay is £345 a week.
20 ONS Data given to the author on request. According to its 2004 Labour Force Survey, 1.7m considered themselves private sector workers and 683,000 public sector.

Under such stymied circumstances, it is little surprise that
Scotland's business growth rate is so low[21] and its contribution to the UK economy has been steadily declining – while
tax-cutting comparable countries like Ireland have been
booming.

Programmed not to care

Scottish ministers are uniquely unconcerned about the
wealth-creating side of the economy because, uniquely for a
country, their budget is not related to the amount of money
generated by its private sector. This is a crucial defect of
devolution.

They are not unduly worried about the worklessness in
Scotland's new ghettos because the bill for this is picked up by
the Department for Work and Pensions in London whose bill
is directly drawn from the UK economy.

The Scottish Executive need not fret about the lost economic input from Third Scotland, because the budget of the
devolved Scottish government is literally driven more by economic activity in south east England than by the economic
prospects of east Glasgow or Dundee.

This was the case long before devolution, where the
government machine based in Edinburgh had no regard for
efficiency and was overwhelmingly concerned with extorting
the maximum amount of money from the UK Treasury.

In her memoirs, Margaret Thatcher described a mood in
her Scottish civil servants which has now become the *leit-
motif* of devolution. 'The pride of the Scotland Office', she

---

21 Bank of Scotland on 17 December 2005 showed 651 businesses per
   10,000 adults against an average across the UK of 846 businesses per
   10,000 adults (i.e. 23 per cent less).

wrote, 'was that public spending per head was far higher than in England.'

This attitude continues today. When under fire for dismal NHS performance or dire economic growth and appalling poverty levels, Scottish Labour ministers repeatedly recite spending figures – as if this is an end in itself.

The figures are indeed extraordinary. In 2006, government spending will equate to 52.8 per cent of Scotland's economic output,[22] pushing it marginally ahead of Finland to fourth place in the league table of OECD industrialized countries. The UK is allocated a lowly seventeenth place.

Normally, countries with high spending feel the pain in high tax. Not Scotland. Of every £4 it receives, at least £1 is donated by other parts of the UK economy. This is due to a system called the Barnett Formula which divides public spending in Britain. Designed in 1978 to prepare for a devolution plan which sank through insufficient support in a 1979 referendum, the Barnett Formula[23] preserves Scotland's historic spending advantage over England and erodes what gets added on top.

The subsidy is English money. In 2002–03, the last year for which figures are available, Scotland generated £40.1bn in taxation revenue and received £31.6bn government spending.[24] The difference is £9.3bn – in effect, the extent to which Scotland is subsidized.

A popular myth in Scotland is that the North Sea oil and gas taxation would fill this gap. But in 2002–03, the entire

---

22 Forecasts by the author, from Fraser of Allander economic projections, ONS data for economic output in UK and from the November 2005 edition of HM Treasury consensus forecasts for deflation and economic growth.

23 An excellent explanation of the Barnett Formula is offered by a House of Commons briefing document number on the subject published on 30 November 2001, ref: 01/108. It can be found on www.parliament.uk/commons/lib/research/rp2001/rp01-108.pdf.

24 Ibid.

North Sea tax haul was £4.9bn.[25] If Scotland kept every penny of North Sea oil, it would still be £4.4bn in the red. The imbalance is getting worse.

When Mr Brown began his public spending bonanza in 2001, his stated aim[26] was to lift UK health spending to standards seen in continental Europe. But Scotland was already at this level – and its spending has been pushed to Scandinavian levels. A future Scotland needs a new Barnett formula with a new system that will introduce a direct link between what is raised in tax and given by the Exchequer in benefits. This will give ministers an incentive to respect the private sector and tackle the ghetto problem.

Such an arsenal of public spending conspires to make the government the dominant player in the Scottish economy. By its own description,[27] 28.4 per cent of the Scottish workforce was employed by the government over 2004, against 24 per cent for the UK as a whole.

Incompetence of ministers

In Scandinavia, the argument is that the state spends this money efficiently – thus turning it into economic growth. But in Scotland, the apparatus is run by MSPs whose enthusiasm for running public services is matched only by their abject lack of qualifications for doing so.

---

25 HM Treasury, Budget 2003.
26 In his 2002 Budget, Brown pledged to lift UK health spending from 7.7 per cent of GDP in 2002–03 to 9.4 per cent of GDP in 2007–08 (p. 121). Subsequent revisions from the ONS, namely the discovery of military and charitable health spending, found that the UK was spending more on health than he realized, and this target would have been met without the extra health spending.
27 Labour Force Survey published by the Office for National Statistics. Data not normally broken down for Scotland, but given to the author on request.

It is an irony of politics that an undistinguished teacher, who may never have made headmaster in school can, by political allegiance, be elected a politician in a safe seat and end up running the entire national education system.

The fiasco over the construction of the Scottish Parliament was only the most visible example of incompetence in government in Scotland. The machine does not work, and a useful rule for a future Scotland is to have it do as little as possible.

The most deplorable example is the National Health Service. In 1997, Scots were asked to elect Tony Blair as Prime Minister on a pledge to reduce waiting lists. He went on to introduce a radical reform agenda, giving NHS contracts to private clinics.

Jack McConnell, Scotland's First Minister, used his devolved powers to tighten his grip over the NHS in Scotland. It was like a controlled experiment: two NHS systems, given the same spending increase, one reforms and the other does not. Who wins?

Scotland's sick have been used as political pawns so the MSPs can make a losing political point. Today, the average waiting list in England has plunged[28] by 25 per cent from 1999 levels. In Scotland, its waiting list has soared[29] by the same figure: 25 per cent.

The average waiting time for an inpatient operation in Scotland now stands at a scandalous 43 days – 11 days more than it was in 1999 and a fortnight longer than in 1991 when NHS Scotland had more people to serve and less than half its current budget.

28 England waiting list fell from 1.07m in 1999 to 795,000 in October 2005. Data from Department of Health website, www.dh.gov.uk.
29 In 1999, Scottish NHS had 90,062 waiting and categorized as inpatient and day cases. By August 2005, this was 112,639 – a 25 per cent rise. Average inpatient wait had risen 34 per cent to 43 days. This and all NHS Scotland performance data can be found on ISD Scotland on www.isdscotland.org.

By any account, this is extraordinary. It shows managerial incompetence of staggering proportions. In Whitehall, English ministers ask how any managers – political or professional – can so spectacularly short-change the sick whose needs they are paid to tend.

The difference? In England, an internal market has been introduced in the NHS and contracts are awarded to new clinics who tackle bottlenecks in the system. In Scotland, the politicians have tightened their grip on NHS Scotland – and signally failed.

It is, alas, not just the NHS they run. MSP ministers are lucky that education cannot be as easily measured. Their record, where it has become evident – in NHS Scotland or the construction of the Scottish Parliament building – is of world-class incompetence.

The same people are running Scotland's council estates – and the lives of the people within them. Having identified incompetence as a hallmark of Scotland's political class, the task is to transfer as much power as possible away from them, and towards the Scottish public.

Health vouchers

The trail has been blazed by the NHS in England. The Scottish Executive seeks to assuage its critics by saying it will adopt the market system working in England, but it is moving at glacial pace. This needs to be accelerated.

Hospitals must sell operations, at a unit price, to those who commission care. If NHS Scotland's prices are higher than the private sector (lack of data currently makes comparison impossible) then new entrants can come and cut a swathe through the waiting list.

We know that the costs per case in Aberdeen Royal

Infirmary have doubled since 1999 – a typical example which suggests that, if operations were put out to tender, they would soon attract the new breed of health firms who would tackle bottlenecks.

NHS Scotland has been separate since its 1945 inception[30] from NHS in England – but its budget has long been higher, partly due to poorer health and partly due to Scotland's success over the last few decades of negotiations with HM Treasury.

Over 2005, planned government health spending was £1,620 a head for Scotland and just £1,300 a head in England. Glasgow, as ever, sets the record. The city's NHS[31] budget was £1,950 per person for 2004/5 – enough to put every man, woman and child onto BUPA.

The money is there. All it needs is the political green light to liberalize the health service, and a new wave of entrepreneurship will come and deliver healthcare to the poorest who need it most – and who suffer the most from the incompetence of the Scottish Executive.

Education vouchers

The next task is to provide exit strategies from the new ghettos. This was once done by grammar schools, which gave

---

30 NHS Scotland was separate at the behest of Joseph Westwood, then Secretary of State for Scotland who produced a separate paper in December 1945. It was inaugurated in July 1948. Its first annual budget was £34.5m for 1949–50, up from the £25m spent privately the year before. In 2005–06, it is £9.1bn.

31 Budget from Greater Glasgow NHS Board, Board Paper No 05/26 printed 22 March 2005. Population under health board is 866,370 in 2003 according to GRO. www.gro-scotland.gov.uk/files/03mid-year-estimates-table2.xls .

bright working-class pupils a special leg up. Many in Middle Scotland credit their social elevation to a good education.

This ladder has been kicked away by the Labour government on ideological grounds. The comprehensive system matches the best state schools to the richest areas: it is selection by house price, under the false guise of equality.

We can see the true state of the system by considering the case of two Glasgow schools: Govan High and Hutcheson Grammar. Both are in the same city, but a world apart. One is an under-performing comprehensive with one of the worst records of results in Scotland – the other is an acclaimed institution with an admissions queue stretching the world over. The difference between them is not money, but politics.

At most, the difference in fees is £33 a week. This is because the amount Glasgow City Council spends per pupil on education is £4,800 a year:[32] fees for Hutcheson Grammar are £6,200. The gap, while tantalizingly close, is unbridgeable for council estate children.

At present, the political and educational establishment in Scotland remains in denial about education inequality. The league table of results is no longer published:[33] yet the old data allows us to trace a direct link between the best exam outcomes and richest areas.

The reason why Castlemilk children do not go to Hutcheson Grammar is not money: the teaching costs are comparable. Nor is it because Castlemilk children are unintelligent. They are directed to sink schools by the political prejudices of Scotland's Left-leaning political elite.

---

32 CIPFA Scotland, Rating Review Estimates of Income and Expenditure 2004–05.

33 While no longer published by the Scottish Executive, it can be extracted by journalists under the Freedom of Information Act and the details given to parents in this way.

The case for school vouchers

There is another way, demonstrated by Sweden. It is one of the many countries to have adopted the voucher system, which makes each child worth a certain amount of money – and creates a market, where new schools can be set up to compete on health and quality.

For a market to work, supply must exceed demand. This it does every year, as depopulation creates thinning classrooms. Rather than close down surplus space, schools can be allowed to compete for children: the sharpest concentration of which lies in the poorest estate.

Due to Scotland's extra public spending, a voucher system would be more valuable than in England. Adopting it for education would address two problems: the extra school places being made every year, and the urgent task of lifting such people out of poverty.

If the system is loaded to favour the poorest, then they could easily have the means to avail themselves of Scotland's world-class private schools. Establishments like Hutcheson could expand, widening their winning formula with a financial incentive to help the poorest.

Would a child want to be bussed from one end of town to the other? Let the parents decide: this is no concern of the politicians. In some parts of urban Sweden, parents are given a brochure of all local schools. Such choice is what Scotland's poorest need.

The task here is to break the link where a child born into Slum Scotland can expect to stay there – and grows up aspiring to claim incapacity benefit in the same way that Middle Scotland's children aspire to go to university.

Education can be made into an industry in Scotland. In Sweden, the voucher system found a generation of teachers who had the ideas to set up their own school in rural areas, where locals had once been bussed to a school deemed large enough by the state.

And the voucher would be worth even more once the local authorities, who control state schools, get out of the picture. There has never been an estimate on how much money intended for schools is absorbed by administration. Suffice to say it can transform education.

In England, education spending is lower, so the economics of its voucher system do not stack up. This is where Scotland's opportunity lies. The voucher system can make the concept of a sink school redundant.

Conclusion

After the French riots in late 2005, the Interior Minister Nicolas Sarkozy made a bleak assessment about life in his own jobless ghettos. They were filled with the combustible combination of young, alienated and mainly Muslim men who saw nothing but unemployment ahead.

The 'sickness in the suburbs' was a reflection of a wider 'malaise', Sarkozy said. 'They are not another France but France as we have built, and managed it, for the past 30 years.' Scotland's ghettos are the result of what Scottish Labour has built and managed for 40 years.

The party held control over Glasgow City Council throughout the Thatcher years. It built and ran the housing schemes. It now seems blind to the fact that an idea that started with the best of intentions is yielding the worst of results.

The priority for a Scottish tomorrow is to clear the ghettos. In a rich country whose unemployment is amongst the lowest in the world, it is a scandal that such appalling deprivation still exists. The problem of Third Scotland must be acknowledged and tackled.

Next, the problem of welfare dependency must be tackled by making Scotland the test case for American-style welfare reform. All incapacity benefit claimants must be reassessed: those able to work should be required to. This is the basic principle of social justice.

Third, control of schools and hospitals must be taken from the Scottish bureaucratic class and handed to the professionals. This can be done by a menu of choice, similar to that described (but not implemented) by Mr Blair in England.

The new principle must be that the government pays for services, but does not provide them. The guiding theme is that the answers for Scotland's rejuvenation do not lie in its political leaders, but in the confidence and the character of the Scottish people. Devolution is a process, not an event. Political power sent from Whitehall in 1999 must no longer be hoarded by MSPs or civil service, but fully transferred to a public whose collective wisdom has for generations been far superior to those political leaders.

Devolution did not mean an enfeebled people swapping one set of political rulers for another. The task for a Scottish tomorrow is to unclench the fist of the state with the 'choice' agenda, and to pursue welfare reform with an agenda of empowerment, not entitlement.

Scotland is a nation of contradictions, but also a nation of genius. There is no reason why it should settle for weak economic growth, ill health, nor accept that inner-city deprivation is somehow inevitable. All this can change, if there is a will to change it.

There is another way. Scotland can be a cradle for new political ideas, not a museum for old ones. To help Scotland, politicians in London and Edinburgh can adopt a simple but radical agenda: to reform welfare, then get out of the way and let the people do the rest.

           *   *   *

Fraser Nelson is Associate Editor of *The Spectator* and Political Editor of *The Business*. He was for five years Westminster Editor of *The Scotsman*, and principal political columnist for the paper. He lives in London.

GILLIAN BOWDITCH

10

Scotland's NHS: Great noise, but where's the motor?

IF THERE IS ONE AREA of Scottish life which should have changed significantly for the better as a result of devolution, it is the National Health Service. Established on 5 July 1948 by a Labour government to provide healthcare for all citizens from cradle to grave, it is one of the greatest social achievements of the twentieth century. The modern-day health service is a very different animal from the NHS established by Aneurin Bevan 57 years ago. But it has, so far, remained true to its founding principle that it should treat people on the basis of need, not ability to pay.

For the Scottish Labour Party the NHS is a touchstone. After all, if the Labour Party in Scotland does not stand for health, what does it stand for? But in the seven years since Labour took control of Scotland, something has gone very badly wrong with the NHS. When a quarter of a million Scots are galvanized into signing petitions demanding that the government 'save our health service',[1] and when MSPs are elected solely on the basis of keeping a local hospital open, it is clear that the service is suffering from a deep

---

1 *Fit For The Future: A National Framework for Service Change in the NHS in Scotland*, published May 2005.

malaise. The ideological battle which is being fought just now is for the very future of the NHS in Scotland.

It is telling that Professor David Kerr, who this year published the latest blueprint for Scottish Health Service, *Fit For The Future*, should feel the need to state emphatically in the first paragraph of his report that 'the NHS is not in crisis'. Yet cancer rates in Scotland are set to rise by 40 per cent in the next decade;[2] the number of Scots aged 80 and over will double in the next 25 years;[3] productivity in the NHS has fallen despite record levels of spending[4] and Scotland's most senior cancer clinician has warned that the strain on NHS budgets and services is so severe that if radical change is not implemented soon, services could deteriorate and senior medical staff move south.[5] Even Kerr admits that 'the status quo definitely cannot be an option'.[6]

Professor Kerr is right in that parts of the Scottish NHS are working extremely effectively. Our breast cancer screening take-up rate is the best in Britain and we vaccinate more elderly people against flu than any other region. On an anecdotal level, plenty of people report excellent service and treatment. Many more are prepared to overlook long hours spent in crumbling waiting rooms because of the dedication, compassion and expertise of staff. But this only serves to expose the great myth of modern-day state medical provision – there is no longer any such thing as a *National* Health Service. Health care in the twenty-first century is a federalized system. Devolution has led to the balkanization of the NHS

---

2   Dr Anna Gregor, lead cancer clinician for Scotland, in an interview in *The Scotsman*, 12 May 2003.
3   *Fit For The Future*, p. 14.
4   *Audit Scotland: An Overview of the Performance of the NHS in Scotland*, published August 2004.
5   Dr Anna Gregor, lead cancer clinician for Scotland, in an interview with *The Scotsman*, 22 June 2004.
6   *Fit For The Future*, p. 2.

and sometimes it seems as if Scots are living in the medical equivalent of Albania.

In the last seven years, Britain has been involved in a huge medical experiment in which we are all guinea pigs by default. Since 1998, England, Scotland, Wales and Northern Ireland have pursued significantly different health policies. Ironically it was a pre-devolution health minister, Sam Galbraith, who took the Scottish NHS down a radically different route from that of England by scrapping the 'internal market' model with its Thatcherite overtones. In his White Paper, *Designed to Care*,[7] Galbraith orchestrated a return to an old-style, directly-managed NHS with an emphasis on integration. In England, despite initial rhetoric denouncing the internal market, New Labour retained it, out-Torying the Tories with the implementation of national targets and performance-related incentives.

The Welsh have gone down a different path from their mainland neighbours with a move away from acute hospital services in favour of longer-term public health and preventative measures. They have concentrated on developing partnerships between the NHS, local authorities and local communities; a direction very much favoured by Professor Kerr's blueprint for Scotland and reinforced by the Scottish Executive's latest ten-year plan for the NHS *Delivering For Health*. Northern Ireland, which always ran its health service rather differently from the rest of the country, has seen its plans stalled by political uncertainty in the last year.

So which of the four models has proved the most successful? A study published in the *BMJ* by the London School of Economics and The King's Fund, analysing health statistics for all four countries pre- and post-devolution, shows that although England had the lowest per capita spending on health and Scotland the highest, England was producing

---

7   *Designed to Care*, December 1997, abolished the internal market and fund-holding in Scotland from 1999.

appreciably better results than anywhere else in Britain.[8]
The results in the reduction in waiting times in England were
particularly striking, although a lack of similarly collated
data for Scotland makes direct comparison in this area
impossible.

At the heart of Scotland's devolved health service is an
almost unfathomable paradox. By 2008 the budget for the
NHS in Scotland will have doubled in a decade to £10.3bn.[9]
Scotland has traditionally spent around 16 per cent more per
capita on health than England. Geography and the poor
health record of Scots dictates that the country employs significantly more medical staff than England. Almost 150,000
people work for the NHS in Scotland – one in every 17 adults
in paid employment in Scotland.

In 2002–03 Scotland employed 30 per cent more doctors
and nurses per head of population than England and has
almost double the number of hospital beds.[10] Yet despite
some significant health gains, notably in mortality rates for
stroke, cancer and coronary heart disease, we are not seeing
anything like the advances investment on this scale should
warrant. It should also be noted that many of the improvements in mortality rates were well on course before the new
money came through and are largely the result of lifestyle
changes. Productivity, as measured by outpatient appointments and inpatient admissions per clinician, has actually
fallen.[11] Why is this?

---

8   'Information In Practice: Effect of diverging policy across the NHS',
    BMJ, 21 October 2005.
9   *Fit For The Future*, p. 8.
10 'Information In Practice', 21 October 2005 (7.4 nurses per 1,000
    population compared with England's 5.6 nurses and 1.8 doctors and
    dentists to England's 1.4).
11 *Overview of the Financial Performance of the NHS in Scotland
    2003/04*. Scottish Parliament Paper 366, June 2005.

Trail back through six years of policy announcements by three Scottish health ministers and one factor stands out; the tendency to implement policy without knowing what the costs and benefits are likely to be. The new consultants' contract is a classic example of this.

Said Dr Andrew Walker of the Robertson Centre for Biostatistics at Glasgow University and one of Scotland's leading health economists, 'When we asked what the cost of the new consultants' contract would be, we were invariably told: "we won't know until it is implemented", but that is no way to run a service.

'The Executive could argue that it had no option but to implement the new contract in line with England but it should have known in advance what the costs were going to be and what we are likely to get for our money. There should have been a specific political judgement that the cost was worth the projected benefit. As a result, it is very unclear what value for money we got out of that deal.'

The NHS in Scotland has been redesigned more often than the Chanel handbag. But when it comes to the financial management of the service, there is no obvious strategy, a legacy perhaps of a nation which does not enjoy its own tax-raising powers and which is dependent on the Barnett formula. NHS targets and goals in Scotland seem to be set arbitrarily, in a vacuum. New policy decisions are made before the preceding policy has been evaluated or in some cases bedded-in. Economics is, at best, an after thought. In his blueprint for Scotland, Professor Kerr pays lip-service to the need for affordability but there is very little space in the report given over to costs.

The Kerr report says his team consulted Dr Andrew Walker at Glasgow University's Centre for Biostatistics and while Dr Walker 'sounded a note of caution in suggesting there was limited evidence of costs and benefits for changes of this

magnitude', the report concludes that the changes it recom-
mends will be cost-neutral for the NHS.[12]

Talk to Dr Walker, however, and a different picture
emerges. 'I put in a 100-page submission', he says. 'The Kerr
report concludes that its recommendations will be broadly
cost-neutral. That is emphatically not what I told them.'

In England, the market drives the system with tightly
defined contracts and payment by results. A national tariff
has been set for operations and other procedures. If a hospital
can carry out an operation for less than the tariff, it gets to
keep the extra money. This is an incentive to undertake as
many operations as efficiently as possible and one of the main
reasons for the dramatic fall in waiting lists south of the
border. The principle of the money following the patient is at
the heart of the system. It is by no means perfect and there
have been problems with its implementation but there is
cohesion and economic logic to the English system.

In Scotland, it is difficult to define what is driving the
system. There is no obvious engine. A report by Audit Scotland discovered that prices for routine treatments varied by as
much as 200 per cent between health boards.[13] Incentives to
innovate and increase productivity are difficult to discern.
The emphasis is on cooperation and collaboration. Most
worrying of all, productivity in Scotland, which had been
ahead of England for much of the 1990s, plateaued in 1999,
at exactly the same time Sam Galbraith's reforms to scrap the
internal market came into effect. Kerr still believes health
improvement can be achieved 'through collaboration and
internal cohesion'.[14] But the evidence from 1998 onwards
suggests otherwise.

---

12 *Fit For The Future*, p. 19.
13 Audit Scotland: *An Overview of The Performance of The NHS in Scot-
    land*, published August 2004.
14 *Fit For The Future*, p. 2.

In the financial year 2004–05, some £752 million of new money will have been poured into the NHS. But £482 million of this will be soaked up by existing policy commitments, such as the new pay deals for clinicians and the cost of new drugs. More than half will have been used just to keep the NHS in Scotland standing still. Despite all the new money, the NHS in Scotland today is carrying out the same number of acute elective procedures as it was five years ago. The new money does not seem to be buying anything more. If the health service in Scotland had kept the rate of productivity growth that it enjoyed in the early 1990s, thousands more operations would be carried out each year.

'The incentive structure for the whole system in Scotland was removed in 1998', says Dr Walker. 'In England, there are financial incentives to push productivity up and real penalties if targets are not met. That is what is driving the improvement in the English statistics. In Scotland, we are relying on people's professionalism to shake up their working practices. If nobody is really pushing for change, then it can be easier to stick with the status quo.'

It is not just clinicians who can be resistant to change. In Scotland, the entire system can mitigate against it so that even the most innovative and forward-thinking clinicians can find themselves thwarted. One Glasgow GP who followed the latest evidence-based advice on prescribing statins to patients with high cholesterol and diabetes found it a thankless task.

His patients were ungrateful because they had been largely symptom-free and as a result of the medical intervention, either suffered minor side-effects or felt unhappy about being on long-term medication. The other partners in the practice were unhappy because the GP had created extra work and tied up the administrative staff. The health board sent round the prescribing advisor who warned the GP that his prescribing of statins was four times the health board average. The incentive to follow best practice in that instance was non-existent.

It is true that, unlike the new consultant contract, the new GP contract does provide financial incentives for meeting targets. Although to the average private sector employee, the concept of being paid extra for what should be a core part of the job is an anathema. And even some GPs are amazed at how easily they have been allowed to opt out of out-of-hours provision. But the Glasgow GP's experience demonstrates that, even with something as simple and uncontroversial as the prescribing of statins, there are many hurdles to be negotiated. The Scottish model as a whole actually provides disincentives for implementing change.

Comparisons with England are illuminating but even when the Scottish NHS is measured against its own limited criteria for improvement, it performs dismally. In 2001, the Executive set 14 targets for the NHS with the aim of improving the health and quality of life of people in Scotland. These range from reducing mortality rates from cancer, stroke and coronary heart disease to reducing waiting times.

Many of the targets, however, are woollier than a flock of Shetland sheep. One states: 'All NHS Boards will demonstrate regular and sustained improvement, as reflected in the reports by NHS Quality Improvement Scotland in performance against the Healthcare Governance Standards set by NHSQIS.' Another calls for all NHS Boards to 'achieve year-on-year improvements in the involvement of the public in the planning and delivery of NHS services'. It's easy to conclude that if a health board involves nobody one year and one person the next, it will by definition have met the target.

A study carried out by Dr Walker[15] found that of the 14 targets, eight were useless as targets, either because perform-

---

15 Unpublished.

ance could not be measured or because what is measured could not be linked to Executive policies. One target (a reduction in the incidence of adults exceeding weekly drinking limits) seems to have been missed altogether; one (a reduction in smoking rates from 35 per cent to 33 per cent in the ten years from 1995) was likely to have been achieved but was disappointing because it was so unambitious. Two (cancer treatment maximum waiting times and primary care maximum waiting times) may have been achieved but data collection was not of adequate quality to ascertain this, despite the Executive having had three years to put a system into place.

Just two (maximum waiting times for outpatient and inpatient treatments) appear to have been met without qualification. During the period that these targets were operational (2002–04) £21.7 billion was spent on health. Two out of 14 is hardly a ringing endorsement of current health policy. 'Arguably the Executive is taking credit for existing trends', says Dr Walker. 'It's like saying: "In May we will make the temperature rise".'

So will the new NHS ten-year plan, *Delivering For Health*, unveiled by the Health Minister, Andy Kerr, on 27 October 2005, change things? The plan is based very closely on the work of Professor Kerr and while there is much in the Kerr report which is praiseworthy, there are two main problems; the Kerr recommendations are not detailed and they have not been properly costed. As a result Kerr can be read in different ways by different people.

The emphasis on community-based hospitals, care in the community and managing disease in a primary care setting could be seen as a vindication of the way Argyll & Clyde Health Board ran its services, but Argyll & Clyde has just been abolished by the health minister after running up debts of £80m.

As for the suggestion that Kerr's recommendations will be cost-neutral, while the emphasis on prevention and managing chronic disease in the community may save money in the longer term, in the short term it is difficult to see how costs will do anything but rise. Community teams cannot fully replace the need for acute hospital services and could end up introducing another tier to the service. A degree of duplication seems inevitable.

Likewise, while Kerr's plan to separate emergency surgery from elective surgery will delight many patients who have suffered repeated cancellations of their operations, it is hard to see how it can be done without increasing the number of surgeons, anaesthetists, nurses and operating theatres. And while the plans to use more pharmacists and retrained nurses may meet with patients' approval in theory, in practice, patients given an appointment with a pharmacist when they expect a consultation with a doctor, may feel fobbed off.

'Kerr could potentially cost a lot to implement', says Dr Walker. 'It is staff numbers which determine the costs of the NHS. Some 70 per cent of NHS costs are labour costs. I'm open to the arguments but I'm not at all convinced that Kerr represents a cheaper or a cost-neutral service.'

If anything, the flurry of government policies means that more staff will be needed to implement them. The BMA's General Practitioners' committee and the Royal College of General Practitioners have calculated that it will require a 30 per cent increase in the UK GP workforce to implement initiatives such as audit, appraisal, chronic disease management and intermediate care. This would mean recruiting an additional 1,200 GPs in Scotland.[16]

The problem with the Kerr report, as with all its predecessors, is that it starts from a position of what sort of NHS we

---

16 BMA Priorities For Health – background briefing December 2002.

want, rather than what sort of service we can afford. What we want is very simple: a healthcare system comparable with the best in the world. But to offer a world-class healthcare system free at the point of delivery would necessitate a phenomenal increase in spending, much higher than the 8 per cent to 10 per cent annual increase pledged by the government to 2008.

Before any new redesign for the NHS in Scotland is implemented, all the existing policy initiatives should be drawn together, costed and their efficacy calculated. We need to put an order of magnitude around the whole thing – a sort of Scottish Wanless report, if you like.

Most important, we have to recognize that there is no level of spending which will meet total demand and so if the principle of an NHS free at the point of delivery – the great shibboleth – is to be maintained (and there is, as yet, no political appetite north of the border for anything else), a move towards paying for outcomes seems inevitable. We need to look at what every NHS pound buys and see if it could be spent better elsewhere in the system. The question we need to ask is: if we put more money in, what are we getting back in terms of health gain? At present there is no real system for measuring quality of life and equating it with cost of treatment. So we have a system whereby thousands of pounds can be spent prolonging the life of a terminally ill cancer patient by a matter of weeks while dozens of hip replacement operations, which could increase a patient's quality of life for years and improve their general health, are postponed.

'The only outcome the NHS really measures is whether somebody is dead or alive', says Dr Walker. 'Florence Nightingale 150 years ago had a system classifying patients as "dead", "relieved" or "not relieved". These days we don't have anything quite as sophisticated as that.'

A system which delivers the most effective healthcare

available for our £10bn would look quite different from a system designed for maximum customer satisfaction; the 'happy patient model' versus 'the healthy patient model'. We have to decide where along that spectrum we want the health service to be. At present, there is rarely even an acknowledgement that these two systems are different. Yet the pressure towards a consumerist 'happy patient' model rather than an efficient 'healthy patient' model remains high because people vote on the basis of whether they are happy, not on the basis of whether they are healthy. A case in point is the way the politicians are succumbing to the idea of providing unevaluated alternative therapies on the NHS because patients are starting to demand them.

The situation is made more acute by our expectations and aspirations in other areas of life. A population used to 24-hour banking and round-the-clock supermarkets, which can have a choice of 50 types of bread and ten types of coffee, is unlikely to feel satisfied with a single procedure, provided by a monolithic state-controlled monopoly at a time and a place of its choosing.

In England, patients are being provided with a system which is significantly different from that on offer in Scotland and appears to offer real patient choice. Under the new Book and Choose system, English patients who visit their GP from 1 January 2006 and are referred for specialist treatment will be able to choose from at least four hospitals or clinics, one of which is likely to be a private provider. They will also be able to select the date and time of their appointment, with the GP eventually booking it online during the consultation. (The technology is a year behind schedule.) Scotland has nothing like England's level of private healthcare and it has geographical problems to overcome, so can patient choice ever work in practice for Scotland?

Dr Walker believes that with the right kind of incentives,

the answer is yes. 'The majority of the Scottish population would have a genuine choice. Most of the rest would have a limited choice which might involve them having to go quite far afield to find an alternative. Only those living in remote rural areas would have no real choice', he says.

So far, nearly all the strategies for the NHS have concentrated on the supply side of the equation, but what about demand? Kerr addresses this problem obliquely by recommending systems which would anticipate acute health 'incidents' before they happen; managing chronic conditions in the community in a more consistent fashion; investing in preventative medicine and by targeting those most at risk of developing chronic long term conditions. All of these ideas seem eminently sensible. But the concept of identifying those at risk before illness strikes could have unforeseen consequences. If we are not careful, The Kerr report and *Delivering For Health* could pander to the Scottish sense of grievance and victimization and turn us into a nation of patients, encouraging us to see ourselves as ill all the time.

There is no shortage of evidence that we are already a nation of hypochondriacs. A survey of 400 family doctors for *General Practitioner* magazine, carried out by Professor Colin Francome of the Department of Medical Sociology at Middlesex University, discovered widespread abuse of the service, north and south of the border.[17] One GP revealed that she is consulted by patients who have run out of baby food or need to change a light bulb. The average GP experiences 18 missed appointments each week, costing the NHS in Britain in excess of £185m.[18]

---

17 'Majority of GPs Now Favour Charging for Consultations', *General Practitioner*, 25 August 2000.
18 Research, carried out by the Doctor Patient Partnership and the Institute of Healthcare Management, quoted in *Medeconomics*, p. 80, 19 October 2000.

For the first time, a majority of doctors have voted in favour of charging a fee for a GP appointment. In England, 52 per cent backed the principle. In Scotland the figure was 34 per cent. Such a charge would be unworkable and un-collectible as well as downright dangerous if it deterred the genuinely sick. But it does highlight the extent of the problem. A generation has grown up in Britain which puts more thought into choosing a take-away pizza than it does into calling the GP's surgery. Until we educate people to use the service responsibly, the pressures will only increase.

The Scottish Executive has mismanaged the system but we, the electorate have abused it, making increasingly frivolous demands on it, failing to keep appointments, refusing to take any responsibility for our own health and wellbeing, eating, drinking and smoking ourselves to death while expecting a beleaguered service to offer ever more expensive and sophis-ticated medications and procedures free of charge.

If our service is to remain free at the point of delivery – and it is worth remembering that in 2000, a MORI poll found that two-thirds of Britons believed that healthcare would no longer be free by 2007 – three things have to happen: the service has to follow the English model and become much more efficient; the Scottish Executive has to invest its health billions much more wisely and demonstrate value for money; and individuals have to take more responsibility for their health and wellbeing. This is not something that will come about through a propaganda blitz or through the appoint-ment of health 'czars'. It will take a carrot and stick approach. Ironically, one motivation may be a health service under so much pressure that people have no option but to look after their own health as best as they can. Let's hope more positive incentives can be developed before then.

The Executive has 18 months to get its act together ahead of the Holyrood election of 2007. By then we will be spending £2,000 a year on the health service for every man, woman and child in Scotland and health will be firmly on the agenda. The electorate will want to know why Scotland is struggling to achieve targets which England is already achieving; why we are doing no more operations than we were five years ago and why we don't have an English-style Book and Choose system north of the border. If team McConnell cannot answer these questions satisfactorily, the health protests we saw during the last Holyrood elections will look tame.

It might be tempting to dream up novel Scottish solutions for the problems of the NHS: tempting but wrong. This is one case where we should acknowledge that what are needed are English solutions for Scottish problems. The English model is certainly flawed and the culture of the NHS in Scotland may be so resistant to change that importing English structures and incentives may prove too difficult. But unless the Executive swallows its pride and bites the bullet, Britain will be left with a two-tier health system, with Scots enduring a significantly less efficient system than their English neighbours.

The last word goes to Dr Walker, who has been tracking NHS policy and funding for two decades. 'I don't think there is the motor in the current system to deliver', he says. 'It's shocking that we've let it drift like this for the last five years. We may not see this level of investment for a long time. It reminds me of North Sea Oil and the windfall we got from that in the 1970s. My fear is that we are just going to let it slip through our fingers.'

Whether Kerr's belief that the NHS in Scotland is not at crisis point is debatable; the fact that there is no other area of public life in which Scots have been so let down by devolution, is not.

*   *   *

Gillian Bowditch is a leading Scottish commentator on health and social policy. She has been a regular columnist with numerous papers including *The Sunday Times* and *The Scotsman*, where she has undertaken extensive research on health issues ranging from alcohol-related problems to cancer treatment. Gillian lives in Stirling.